Eugenio Montale

The Butterfly
of Dinard

Translated by G. Singh

The University Press of Kentucky

Lexington   1971

Standard Book Number 8131-1252-4

© Arnoldo Mondadori Editore

This translation © London Magazine Editions, 1970

United States edition published 1971 by
The University Press of Kentucky

A statewide cooperative scholarly publishing agency serving
Berea College, Centre College of Kentucky, Eastern Kentucky
University, Kentucky State College, Morehead State University,
Murray State University, University of Kentucky, University
of Louisville, and Western Kentucky University.

Editorial and Sales Offices: Lexington, Kentucky 40506

Printed in Great Britain

2 parts

Contents

Preface   5

PART I
A Stranger's Story   9
The Yellow Roses   14
Donna Juanita   19
The Regatta   24
The 'Busacca'   29
Laguzzi and C.   33
The House with the Two Palm-trees   36
The Bearded Woman   42
In the Key of 'Fa'   47
Success   51
Il lacerato spirito . . .   55
The Ostrich Feather   58
The Best Comes Last   63

PART II
The Enemies of Mr. Fuchs   69
Mr. Stapps   72
Dominico   76
Alastor's Visit   80
Honey   83
Clizia at Foggia   88
The Stormy One   93
The Women of Karma   98
The Slow Club   101

PART III

The Bat   107

The Angiolino   112

The Relics   116

The Russian Prince   120

'Would you like to change yourself into . . .?' 123

A Difficult Evening   125

The Red Mushrooms   127

The Ash   129

The Producer   133

The Widows   136

The Culprit   138

Poetry Does Not Exist   143

PART IV

The Man in Pyjamas   151

An English Gentleman   153

Sul Limite   156

On the Beach   162

The Paintings in the Cellar   167

Anguish   171

The New Year's Eve Dinner   175

The Condemned   179

The Flight of the Hawk   181

The Snow Statue   184

The Butterfly of Dinard   186

Preface

After ten years of unemployment due to political reasons—I didn't belong to the 'Party'—I joined in 1948 the editorial staff of an important Milanese daily. This, owing to the shortage of paper, as of everything else, used to come out in two or four page editions only. The editor's idea was that I should leave literature alone. There was no question of my being sent out as a foreign correspondent, since others were already doing that job. But, still, I had to write something. What? I haven't got the imagination of a born novelist; nor can I invent anything. But being a great admirer of the English essayists and having the sense of humour that is seldom wanting in the Ligurians—I was born at Genoa where I lived till I was thirty—I thought that I could perhaps talk about myself and my experiences, without boring readers with the actual autobiography of an ordinary man—a man who has always tried to move through the history of his times in a clandestine way.

This is how these short stories—*culs de lampe*—of *The Butterfly of Dinard* came to be written. Only a few are set in Liguria, but a great many take place in Florence where I lived for twenty years in close contact with the English colony, which in those days was quite large. During those years I tried to do something impossible—to live in Florence like an Italian, exposed to all sorts of vexations from the political regime; and at the same time to live like a foreigner, aloof from local troubles. After something like twenty years of hard but unsuccessful struggle I gave up. In the meanwhile I had moved to Milan—the centre of business, not art. I had brought along with me a long trail of memories which demanded written expression. If I was not a born story-teller, so much the better; if the space at my disposal was limited, better still. This forced me to write in great haste. To cater for the taste of the general public, which is little accustomed to the allusive and succinct technique of the *petit poème en prose*, created no problem.

To write about those silly and trivial things which are at the same time important; to project the image of a prisoner who is at the same time a free man: in this, if I may say so, lies whatever merit these instantaneous flashes which are *The Butterfly of Dinard* may have. These stories *in nuce* were published in book form in 1956; extra stories were added in the subsequent editions of 1961 and 1969. When they first came out they received the general approval of the public as well as of the critics. But perhaps it is only today that, in their English garb, they can be read and appreciated by a different and, I hope, larger public. Some might even think that, thanks to their learned translator, they have at last found a more congenial habitat. Which would no doubt be partly true, although one has to remember that from the age of the Enlightenment onwards Italian has enriched itself with such possibilities as would make it second to none. Perhaps it would need other and bigger Butterflies (written by others) to confer on our national prose—poetry has already made considerable advances in that direction—that flexibility which too illustrious a literary tradition in the past has prevented it from achieving.

EUGENIO MONTALE

Part I

A Stranger's Story

'Perhaps you remember having seen *L'amico della famiglia* at my house? One Saturday morning the postman handed me through the bars of the railing our copy of that innocuous little review—I do not know whether it belonged to a parish or to a mission—to which a certain aunt of mine from Pietrasanta had become a life subscriber. I opened it, glanced anxiously through the puzzles column, and announced in a triumphant voice: Buganza!

'From within the house my father uttered a groan of profound satisfaction.

'Amongst so much discord between my father and myself we had at least one thing in common—a thread that bound us together—namely that at the end of every week the name of the archpriest Buganza would turn up among the "solvers" of the logographs, the picture puzzles and the rebus of the *Amico* (from among which an edifying book would be drawn by lot as a prize). To that harmless mania of the old ecclesiastic, who would have thought it a dishonour not to respond to that weekly appeal, vaguely corresponded our own mania of waiting hopefully for something—a hope that was always fulfilled. In those days there were no cross-word puzzles. But what happened showed that there could be cross-word destinies. Let me tell you the rest of the story.

'I don't know whether it was my father or I who first got interested in that rather odd affair. The archpriest was a complete stranger to us. He didn't live in our city, nor did we bother to find out anything about him. . . . That he was an old man was merely our supposition. The fact is that for years (how many?) his name had invariably appeared in that list, so that he had by now become an essential part of us, a part of our jealous habits. What would he have thought had he known that he himself had helped widen the rift between us? Perhaps he might have regarded it as the work

9

of an evil spirit. And yet it was something that served as a strong link between us. The city was changing its face—exposing itself to the evil influences of modern life. Bars gave way to cafés, frequented by strange youths in bowler hats and frock coats, eating potato crisps day in and day out and drinking Vermouth, if not cocktails as yet. Even theatres were caught up in this ferment of change—theatres where the Viennese operas had replaced the *Gran Via, Boccaccio* and other such means of entertainment known to our forefathers. There were no *girls* as yet, but the variety show, with its stars and singers, and the first cinematic efforts were opening up immense possibilities of corruption for the young. even I, who did not frequent these places, had attached to my mirror a newspaper cutting of that popular actress for whose sake the name of a responsible European monarch had to be changed one fine morning into that of Cleopoldo. When my father came across that cutting a violent quarrel broke out. I threatened to pack up and leave for good.

'But I had no money and in any case how could I leave on a Friday without waiting for news of the archpriest? Next morning Buganza turned up to seal—*in hoc signo!*—our reconciliation.

'Thus our life continued unchanged. Just as Buganza had kept us together for months he continued to do so for years. My father lived partly at home, partly in his office, where he was helped by my brothers who really were independent; whereas I spent all my time between home and the arcades of the new streets—still unemployed. Not, of course, that I wasn't always on the look-out for a job—a job worthy of me and my talent. But neither I nor my father had ever discovered what that talent was. In a family like ours, as a matter of course, one son, usually the youngest, was supposed to be the favourite, and from him no serious occupation was expected. The youngest son of a widower, who had been in poor health since infancy, but who had nevertheless plenty of vague and indefinable ideas about extra-commercial vocations, I had reached the age of fifteen, then twenty, then twenty-five, without ever having taken any decision. I was snatched from home by the war. With its aftermath came the crisis of the great revolution which was meant to save us from the horrors of Bolshevism. Our business affairs went wrong. It was impossible to obtain import permits unless one made a point of forgetting thick envelopes in the offices of "Commendatori" in Rome. But Buganza kept turning up as usual, so that there was at least something stable in our life—something that *held*.

'One Saturday morning there was a serious quarrel between me and my father. Some louts had slapped me on the street because I didn't raise my hand to salute a black-shirt and my old father thought that they had been right and that my folly deserved nothing better. At that very moment *L'amico della famiglia* arrived. I opened it unsuspectingly, only to come upon something quite incredible—something that was going to change the whole course of our life: *The name of Buganza was no longer there!*

'Good-bye Buganza!—I exclaimed after a short pause. I went to my room and started getting ready to leave. I had decided that the break must come now; the thread was broken, the chain was severed; the "ground bass music" called Buganza had gone out of our life; anything could change, was bound to change.

'A new life was starting and it didn't matter whether I knew where or how. My father dealt with this crisis in a dignified manner, making no comment. But I could see that while he was watering the dahlias in the garden he was more depressed and preoccupied than usual, even though he hadn't the faintest clue about my decision to leave. I worked all day, part of the night and the day after, destroying old papers (even the cutting of Cléo de Mérode which I had come upon again after so many years), and packing away others. I had made up my mind, so what was there to fear? By the following Saturday I would no longer be at home, and in any case what difference could it make even if the priest-phantom reappeared? By breaking the rhythm and failing to keep his promise, Buganza had become a dummy in my life, so that I could now dispense with him. Having thus forestalled all eventualities I felt myself completely invulnerable. I actually enjoyed the time that preceded my departure— sipping it bit by bit. I retraced the streets of my infancy one by one, following the routes I had taken for years on my way to school. I had no friends but I took care to pay a few visits and take leave of people (though without hinting about my departure). Nevertheless everyone was rather mystified by my odd remarks. I told my father that I had to go away for a few days, and I'm not sure if he suspected anything. During the whole week I exchanged only a few words with him.

'To tell the truth, the few days before my departure passed almost without my noticing them. I hadn't realised that a new Saturday had come round again until I heard the postman whistle at the gate and saw the green-coloured *Amico* right under my nose. I opened the magazine nonchalantly. What did it matter whether the phantom was there or not? The name, in fact, had returned to its place, but accompanied by a note that dealt me an unexpected blow. "We are sorry", it said, "that on account of a slip on the part of our usually diligent compositor the name of the Very Reverend Arch. D. F. Buganza was omitted from the last number. We offer him many apologies, etc., etc."

'*L'amico della famiglia* slipped from my hand. After a bit I went over to my father, who was immersed in the reading of *Caffaro*, and said:

'—You know, he has come back.

'—Who? Buganza?

'—Yes. Buganza. And it wasn't his fault that he wasn't there last time. It was a printing error. I thought it was rather odd.

'—So did I — my father said, with a sigh of relief.

A little later I started unpacking. There was no way out. The thread I had thought broken proved stronger than ever. And now that my father is no more and the *Amico* has disappeared and the archpriest likewise, my house still stands and only a bomb could . . . but not for the moment I daresay. Did you hear that? The alarm has started again. We can go up now.'

The hoarse sound of the siren, a faintly subsiding *fa*, came in fact from outside. I saw the stranger get up, take his friend by the arm, and walk away to wind up his story in the open.

The Yellow Roses

— Let's imagine you're my secretary — Gerda said to Filippo, looking at him through her *loupe*. — Instead of our meeting by chance in this boarding house a couple of hours ago, suppose you replied to my little advertisement and I have to put you to a test. No, I'm not really going to do that, it's just an experiment I want to conduct after I've heard you talk. It's four o'clock or so; by eight o'clock I should have sent by air mail an exquisitely feminine short story which will appear in twenty-five American magazines at the same time. Nine hundred words, or a thousand at the most. Unfortunately I haven't got a particularly feminine spirit — and she proudly threw back a millet-coloured fringe — and so in cases like these I have to turn to a man. You seem the right sort. How? You don't like literature? Did you never study it? So much the better, that's what's needed. Try to draw on your memory for a nice Italian story. Isn't there anything in the room or in the view outside that reminds you of something important, no matter how old or recent, pleasant or unpleasant? Don't think too hard about it; if it's there, let it come spontaneously.

— Yes, I've thought of something — said Filippo, pointing to a beautiful bunch of flowers in the vase. — But it's only a trifling detail. Those red flowers have made me think of some roses, yellow roses, which I couldn't take home for fear of arousing suspicion and jealousy.

— Yellow flowers — mused Gerda as she half-closed her eyes. — That's what I want. You call that trifling? If it had been, you wouldn't have remembered it. Who gave them to you?

— A poor lame girl in the cathedral square in M. Let me tell you the whole story.

— But just tell it as it comes.

— It's a foggy day. We're waiting for our maid, both the humble victim and the tyrant who had been with us up to the very brink of the disaster. We have come to see her.

14

On our arrival, we phoned her from the station and arranged to meet her. Would she come? She must do the washing first, and then find some excuse for coming out. She is not like the charlady in the canteen who wears a hat; she never goes out. So I wonder if it was a good thing to have given her an appointment at half past two in the afternoon in a big foggy square?

Theodora (suppose that's the name of my wife) will be tried of standing and waiting. But no, not at all; she even suggests that we go to the tram stop at San Clemente, the suburb five miles away where Palmina lives. But is it advisable to leave this place? There's some discussion, some little quarrel (actually I don't know if the quarrel really took place).

— Well, we are in Italy, so you can add a few quarrels — said Gerda — go on.

— Eventually we compromise. I'll walk round the square behind the church, and Theodora will wait here. She promises not to move. In the fog, shadows, brokers and merchants move in the distance. I stroll around the church under the arcades. Let me briefly relate why I was so nervous at the thought of seeing Palmina again. And what if she didn't come? In the struggle for love he who escapes wins. . . . And even though it wasn't actually a matter of love, perhaps Palmina might be shrewd enough to apply the poet's adage to her own case. Perhaps she knows that we missed her a lot during my illness. But it was no longer possible to live with her. She gave everybody hell—Theodora, the shopkeepers, the porter. When Theodora was away she used to sing at the top of her voice 'senza un soldo per dormir—senza un soldo per mangiar—non mi resta che . . .' But what? One's memory! Then she fell ill with bronchitis and thought she was cured, but the doctor thought otherwise. She put the whole question to us in the form of an ultimatum. No convalescence at our expense—either she leaves the hospital and comes back to us, or she goes home. The English were at the gates of the city, and by now we had even stopped keeping count of the bombardments. She came home all of a sudden, quite exhausted by her heavy bundles. At once a quarrel broke out; it was difficult for me to act as peacemaker, so I let her go. For those of us who remained there began that dark period known as the liberation. Hunger, disease, all sorts of disasters. Perhaps Palmina was lucky enough to have escaped in time behind the Gothic line. After a year we heard from her. She had actually left a couple of hours after the quarrel and had managed to find a place on a truck which was later blown up by a bomb on the Apennines. When she reached home she was left with only a shift. When we heard from her again, a semi-clandestine correspondence started between me and her, between her and Theodora, at times menacing, at times affectionate. Would she come back and stay with us? In any case the threads between us were unbroken.

I keep walking aimlessly round the cathedral, come back and find Theodora asking a guard about the tram from San Clemente. Then a tiny figure emerges from the fog and the two shadows get merged into each other in a long embrace. It's her—Palmina—holding out a big roll of paper that ends in a bunch of yellow flowers. The two women set off and I follow them with this mysterious tube in my hand. We look for a café. Palmina never comes to town, so she doesn't know any; but at last we manage to find one, an enormous deserted place next to the billiard-rooms. The two women talk, embrace each other, quarrel and then make up again; in the meantime what looks like the stem of the bunch of flowers is a bottle of wine for me, the roses being for Theodora. Red sparkling wine of Sorbara. I thank her with some embarrassment. Theodora decides she has a couple of things to do. Palmina offers to go with her, but I can't walk in this thick fog with a bottle and a bunch of roses in my hand. I decide to wait at the café. I wait for an hour—sitting alone in a corner full of sawdust among the shadows of the players. Palmina seems to have recovered: her cheeks have a pleasant ruddiness (powder,

16

says Theodora), and there's a kind of grace about her limp. God knows what these two have found to talk about. Actually it's just as well they left me alone here. Women are so inept at reviving old times. Left to myself, I can enjoy this plunge into a life I thought had ended for ever. Will it start again? Nothing starts again. Palmina was very shrewd, especially about the way she speculated on my natural instinct to consider myself always in the wrong. Being herself a natural mistress in the extreme, she would always say 'we poor maid-servants', and I really thought she was ill-treated. In fact it was only her figure that was deformed, for she herself was quite attractive, mainly because of her extraordinary vitality—like a lizard who gets her tail back every time it's chopped off. But she had this about her that in her company even people who were not restless at all felt more restless than she, who was herself so restless. Only stupid people, *nouveaux riches*, and the governesses who speak with the 'r r r', could not understand why we kept her at all. It was something of a scandal for the whole neighbourhood. I look at my watch; there are only twenty minutes before the express leaves; shall we catch the train, or shall we have to stay at M. till midnight, with a bottle and a bunch of roses in my hand? Ah, there's no need to worry, here they are, half irritated, half lingering in each other's embrace. There's still time, so we hurry out. Palmina helps us into a crowded tram, and comes along with us to the station. I look at the clock; it would be a real miracle if we could catch the train. (What on earth can these two women have plotted? I feel both eager and apprehensive that Palmina might decide to come back to us. However, I shall get to know how things stand in the train. There's no time now.)

We arrive at the station, I rush to get a platform ticket for Palmina, and now we're under the roof of the platform as the express draws in. A lot of confusion, embraces, etc. I embrace her, too, for the first time, then we wave from the window as the train starts moving. We have to stand and at a sudden jolt the bottle slips from my hand and rolls to the ground, decapitated. A sweetish pungent smell fills the whole corridor. Everyone's looking at me distastefully, trying to get their feet out of the way of the wine that flows down towards the luggage. The train accelerates; it's dark and cold. Theodora has found herself a seat and remarks that the bottles given by that mad woman had always got broken. After an hour and a half, the express is nearing our destination. 'Now don't think you're going to take those roses home,' says Theodora, 'otherwise our latest dish-washer will suspect we have been to M. to see the viper again, and quit. Keep it under your hat. Offer the roses to Professor Ceramelli who's standing over there at the end of the corridor: offer them for his wife who'll appreciate it. And don't, for goodness sake, tell him we can't take them home.'

The professor—a respectable man whom I haven't seen for ages—is amazed at this unusual present. He can't understand the gesture and hesitates, so I have to invent some sort of excuse, but he's hardly convinced. However he finally decides to accept them, especially as he hasn't got any luggage. The train arrives, there's no longer any fog, he takes his leave and proceeds on his way, flowers in hand. For a few seconds I can still see the pale reflections of a neon inscription on the faint glow of the yellow flowers. Then in the dissolving mist . . . Perhaps that will do? With a bit more order, perhaps . . .

— No, with a bit more disorder — said Gerda looking at her watch — It's a pity I don't have my dictaphone. But in a couple of hours I shall begin my first 'Italian' story. The Yellow Roses: it's the title that counts. Thanks a lot.

Donna Juanita

The intermittent buzz of a radio was audible through the open window. Gerda closed it impatiently and turned towards Filippo, eyes half closed like a tiger in wait for its prey.

— You're not going to leave me now—are you?—since the first experiment came off so well. I need another Italian *suite* for my series. Isn't there anything in the room—paintings, books, crockery, flowers, photographs—that puts you in the right frame of mind? Just relax; I want something absolutely spontaneous. Spontaneity, as you know, is not my strong point.

— No — said Filippo — apart from you, nothing in this place means anything to me. But outside, outside! You can't imagine what sort of person you've shut out of the window.

— Who could it be? — asked Gerda curiously as she looked out on the street. — Someone who wanted to rape me?

— No. A woman: *Donna Juanita*. The music that you abruptly stopped was her: or rather the tune of Suppé's comic opera *Donna Juanita*. But it is she herself that the music has brought back to my mind.

— Your first love? — asked Gerda.

— No, it was something more lasting than that. At first an infantile hatred, then manly pity; and then oblivion . . . that is up to a minute ago, when this tune came back to me.

'Donna Juanita used to come down to the beach for a swim, about midday, wrapped up in a large bathing towel and with a large straw hat tied at the throat. Dark, plump, she didn't like to be looked at, so when she had undressed in the only cabin that was there, she seemed even more dressed than before. Skirt, petticoat—coming down to the ankles—gloves, cord shoes, dark glasses, and hat replaced by a dark turban —all this got inflated by the water and made her look not like a bather, but like an enormous Medusa. Instead of swimming, she would sit on the water, and float about with considerable dignity. The beach sloped rather steeply and everyone knew that after a couple of yards one could no longer touch. But she had a well-planned route. With one wriggle of the tail she would reach the first rock, the *carregún*, as it was called, because of its shape. She would sit there, slippers in the water, gazing proudly at her terrace, which hung over the sea. From here she would again slip into the bosom of the sea (the only bosom visible in the circumstances), the tails of her dress stretching out behind her and carrying her to the "little rock", which represented the second stage, and then on to the "middle rock", a sort of low platform, almost an atoll, bristling with chestnut-husks. But even there, still half in and half out of the water, Juanita would remain only a short while, since some ten-yard swim away there was the final stage to be reached—the "big rock", towering like a pyramid, from the top of which one could see her grand cream-coloured villa which was constructed out of dynamite and money.

'The stages for the return trip were the same, only in the reverse order. Once she got back to the beach, Juanita would wrap another bath-towel around her, before her voluminous costume could deflate to a human shape. Then she would climb back up the pebbled path to her house. Behind her an obliging *criada* would close the gate that was the colour of bull's blood. How old could Juanita possibly be? Perhaps less than forty.

'From the top of the pine-wood overlooking her garden I used to spy on her and her two young daughters—Pilar and Estrellita—sipping *maté* and reading *Caras y Carjetas* and *Scena Illustrata*—the only publications that found their way into this household. Her husband Don Pedro didn't even read those. He had a long smooth moustache and a shaven chin and he used to stroll on the terrace with his Panama hat and gaudy ties and shirts made of raw silk. His favourite occupation was watching the construction of the family burial-ground. He wanted it to be built of Carrara marble, with lots of spires, as befitted his family status. For quite some time they had as their guest a sculptor from Pietrasanta, who was to design the great Neptune and other sea deities on whose shoulders rested the enormous oyster-like terrace. But constantly battered as they were by the stormy sea and the south-west wind, these statues lost every now and then a foot, or a hand, with the result that the work of construction and reconstruction went on for years. The whole thing resulted in an interminable law suit, for Don Pedro who suddenly developed a mania for politics, decided to represent his own constituency as a candidate for the party in power. He narrowly lost the election to a radical candidate, although the latter had spent much less money than Don Pedro. Hence Don Pedro was no longer in a position to maintain his hungry artist. All this was quite unbearable for Don Pedro de Lagorio (please change the name), who ended up in a lunatic asylum and died soon after, raving.

'From then on the sillabub-coloured villa remained closed. Donna Juanita took the children (her *cocorite* as she used to call them) away with her, and left for Boca, the Italian suburb of Buenos Aires, where Don Pedro had made his early fortune.

'You ask if she had gone home? No, her real home was in Italy and even Don Pedro was Italian. He arrived at Boca when still a boy and after having made enough *scaglie*, he imported, so to speak, his Gioannina from his native town in order to marry her. She was his cousin, and he had only seen her in a photograph. The transformation of Gioannina into Donna Juanita took place there, during those years spent in an *avenida* of shop-keepers, where one used to talk the jargon of Cicagna or of Borzonasca rather than *criollo*. It was over there that she emerged from the chrysalid into the fat butterfly that she was. And although she had half-forgotten her native dialect and almost wholly forgotten Italian (which she hadn't known well in any case), she never managed to learn the new language. In Italy she had always been a prisoner, either at home or in the convent. She knew nothing about life at all. She had learnt her favourite music as a child, when at the

21

puppet theatre she used to listen to "Il diluvio universale, con Barudda calafato" (Barudda, you can explain, is a sort of Ligurian buffoon). In this play even God used to have a part in the form of an eye inserted into a cardboard triangle. From the centre of the pupil a ray of light, produced by a wavering candle, would dart out and at that moment an automatic piano would replace the song of the angels with the air of the three highwaymen in *Gran Via*.

'As you see, I learnt about Donna Juanita's past when she was no longer alive. I have even found the *zarzuela* that sealed her destiny. She returned to the villa after the flight, not with three, but with two highwaymen. She had, for the time being, plugged the hole in her capsizing vessel, and her daughters, who were now married, came back to live with her. *El casamiento ingenioso!* But the illusion was short-lived. The two sons-in-law, Ramirez and Bertrán, tall, greedy and with long side-whiskers, made havoc of everything that was left, holding the three women prisoner and heaping blows and abuse on them. Terrible scenes took place in the breakfast-room with its portraits of the great Presidents—from the Mexican Porfirio Diaz onwards—each with an autograph. And when there was nothing left to sell or smash, all three left "for the Americas" (as their countrymen used to say) where they led a rather sad life and met an even sadder end. Donna Juanita was the first to die. She wanted to hang herself because she was afraid of finding the celestial *carregún* she aspired to, occupied; perhaps she got there, to the accompaniment of the tune of the *Cavaliere di grazia*, if the *Gran via* had left any other mark on her. I don't think, however, that her daughters aspired to anything either in life or death. They hadn't really got any home or country, any language or family, which they could call their own. They could never really live a proper life, and perhaps they didn't even suspect that there could be any existence other than their own. I can't imagine who lies in that family tomb constructed at such expense and labour. Perhaps other lunatics in the family, relations of some sort;

22

or perhaps the artist himself came to take possession of his own work.

'Is that enough for you? I know you'd like to know the exact place, beach and spring-board from which Don Pedro took a leap towards the New World: would like to introduce a sharply-drawn picture of the child who hid himself behind a bush in order to throw a pebble at Donna Juanita and her *cocorite*, whom he considered guilty of having constructed a palace worthy of Semiramis, in the inlet where for years there had been only one house—that of his own father. You would like to know in what part of the earth, inhabited by prisoners, criminals and alcoholics, such tales were still possible towards the beginning of a century that had not yet put aside the mask of prosperity and progress. You would like to know . . .'

— Oh, not for the sake of writing it — Gerda protested, while scrawling the title of the story on a piece of paper: *Upstarts* — Come and see me again. . . . Who knows one day I may even be able to offer you a cup of maté. But don't flatter yourself: my resemblance to Donna Juanita would stop there.

The Regatta

Verdaccio—a tiny sea-port protected by high rocks, in the heart of a semi-circle of old houses huddled together or merely divided by narrow passages and winding alleys—was almost in line with Zebrino's room on the third floor of the Montecorvo villa where his family used to spend the summer months. But it was on the opposite side of the inlet, about three miles as the crow flies; and in consequence of the ragged and picturesque bustle of the place one would have needed a pair of binoculars to bring into sharper focus the soot of that lair of pirates and hawks, which not even the Saracens had ever dared approach. No trains stopped there, nor was it accessible by any usable road. There were neither hotels nor rooms to let. If by any chance a stranger happened to land there and ventured out in those lanes he was sure to have full chamber-pots emptied on his head from the top floors, without even the ritual warning 'vitta ch'er beuttu!' (Watch, I am going to throw!)—a cry reserved only for persons of consequence.

So much for the legendary character of Verdaccio which Zebrino continued to regard as a hole in the distant cliffs, a large leafy tree, perhaps a walnut, defying distance and growing almost on the port, or the white spot of a turreted house standing aloof on a rock to the east. That house belonged to the Ravecca family, the squires or at least the undisputed masters of the place—people who could afford to send their children to the technical school in the chief provincial town, who even on week-days would wear shoes, and who used to read papers and spend the winter in the city. In short, they were all quite different from the other people of Verdaccio— women dressed in silk but always barefoot, hairy mysterious men, hand-to-mouth sailors, owners of vineyards without vines, and smugglers.

But did the Raveccas ever exist? Zebrino had never met them. Between Montecorvo and Verdaccio there was little love lost; nor was there much similarity between their dialects either. For not only were the customs of the inhabitants different but also the expressions used by the people of Montecorvo as they threw their by-products out of the windows. However, there was one thing about which Zebrino was quite sure: that some thirty years ago his father was almost engaged to a member of the Ravecca family, the youngest daughter, who was now a widow with many children and who lived in a sort of desert at Fivizzano. She must have been a wretched domestic martyr, penniless and in no way superior to Zebrino's own mother. But this piece of information having filtered down to the boy through a complicated game of allusions, hints and petty squabbles between his parents, could not help producing a certain impression on him. Had things happened in a different way, Zebrino would have been born over there, in that white tower, and Verdaccio would have exercised none of its mysterious spell over him. If his father had married another woman, Zebrino would have been another Zebrino, or rather he would not have had that name at all. . . . Would he have been better or worse off?

The habitual sycophants of his family, those beggars who came in a procession every Saturday to his house, the vagabonds of Pontremoli, who would even stop at Verdaccio, and Battibirba, the mendicant friar who came all the way from Sarzana for the sake of money, took good care to emphasise how Zebrino's father was so much richer and more generous than any of the Raveccas, all of whom had died some years ago, heavily in debt. But the elder Zebrino didn't particularly appreciate allusions to a possible decline of the Raveccas. He did not want people to mention in less than favourable terms the sort of standing he had narrowly missed in his youth. Above all he did not want to be divested of a weapon—the weapon of 'if'—with which he systematically blackmailed the faithful companion of his life. Not that he didn't see eye to eye with his wife; but if the 'trenette col pesto' was not well oiled and seasoned with the Sardinian 'pecorino' cheese, or if the turnip-tops seemed to him to be stuffed with panada instead of pine-seeds and sweetbread, Zebrino's father would always get up on his hind-legs, and pointing towards the house on the other side of the inlet, would make it plain that there, yes over there, such things would never have happened.

Over the years the myth of the Ravecca gradually lost its hold on the child, who was caught up by more exciting occupations. But even before this, the myth was destroyed by an incident, whose hidden significance he alone among the protagonists realised.

On September the 20th each year there used to take place a rowing-regatta at Montecorvo, which was invariably won by the Lampo, the boat belonging to the Zebrinos. It was nimbler than any other boat because of its tapered shape and high prow, which drew very little. At the very first stroke of the oarsmen it would make a yard, thus gaining half a yard's advantage, and making it practically impossible to be overtaken. But that year—Zebrino was twelve—a new rival loomed on the horizon. The Grongo, the fishing boat of the Raveccas, rowed not by the mythical owners, but by three muscular fishermen from Verdaccio, came to compete for the first time. After the usual preliminaries—the greasy pole, the sack-race and the anti-clerical discourse of the anarchist Papiro Triglia—six prows appeared on the horizon waiting for the starting shot. The racing distance was about a hundred yards off the beach, just by the first rocks. A crowd had gathered on the beach, and Zebrino, his brothers and his parents followed the event from above, through the balustrade of their terrace. The Lampo or the Grongo? The Lampo was entrusted to four local veterans: three oarsmen and one helmsman. Even here the honour of the family was not directly involved. But Zebrino was excited about it and even his parents were a bit nervous. Far out one could see the prows jostling each other, the tall, red and white prow of the Lampo and the low, dark green, sinister-looking prow of the Grongo: they were the first and the third from the left. All of a sudden the pistol shot was heard, followed by the simultaneous sound of the first strokes. For some time the boats seemed to be exactly level. The binoculars changed hands, but no one could focus the lenses. The boats seemed stationary, with something plushy about the movement of the oars. Tiny craft, canoes and swimmers bustled around the finishing-post, where Papirio Triglia, the 'authorities', and the jury were stationed.

It was five o'clock in the afternoon. The sun was still shining on the vast arc of the sea between Mesco and the promontory of Monasteroli. One could see the smoke of a goods-train coming out of a deep tunnel in the rocks. And the sporadic curses and rhythmic movement of the oars made the silence of the sea seem even deeper.

— The Lampo — Zebrino's mother said with some confidence as she removed the binoculars from her nose — has gained a yard — she heaved a sigh of relief.

— Possibly — said Zebrino's elder brother, improvising a sort of binoculars by twisting his fingers tightly together. — But this time it's going to be touch and go.

— Let's hope those rogues are really going to give it everything — murmured the other brother, shielding his eyes with the palm of his hand.

— Uhm! — grunted Restin, the bailiff's son, keeping his yellow eyes riveted on the prow of the Lampo. — It's too low in the water today. It's getting on a bit, too.

The boats all seemed stuck together. The cursing oarsmen and helmsmen were bent double in the same position. Half the course must have been covered already.

— Those Verdaccio fellows are pulling like bull-terriers — said the father, trying to focus the binoculars. — I'm afraid we've had it this year. — And he glanced indifferently towards the white spot in the distant landscape.

— We're beaten — Restin agreed, straining his eyes and biting his nails. — The Grongo is doing better. Its crew is lighter.

— You can't be sure yet — said Zebrino's mother turning her eyes away.

— I told you — his father insisted in a moment of irritation. —
No — he added — one can't be quite sure, it's only a matter of
inches.

They could hear the roar from the crowd. The Lampo and
the Grongo, the high prow and the hidden prow, were cutting
their way through the spray, well ahead of the others. The
shouts of the helmsmen were loud enough to drown the splashing
of the oars. Perhaps fifty or thirty yards remained. It seemed
an eternity, and Zebrino's heart was at breaking point. There
was a sharp cry.

— Oh the Lampo! — Restin did a pirouette like a squirrel
as the red prow veered round under the strings of the helm
and the three oarsmen dived into the sea, as was the custom
with the winning crew. Half-drowned among the high waves,
the Grongo, too, reached the winning-post and the Verdaccio
crew defeated but not convinced, hurled venomous insults
against the jury and the boats of the spectators.

— The Lampo — said Zebrino's mother proudly. — It's no
joke beating it.

— Just by a hair's breadth — his father remarked teasingly,
wiping the sweat from his brow. — It's the last time I entrust
it to those drunkards. And now we have to pay for their drinks
too. Are you happy Zebrino?

His hand against his heart, the ashen-faced boy made no
reply. His face was turned towards the east, his eyes fixed on
the white rectangle dominating Verdaccio.

*Childhood disappointments. Apart from
his family.*

*3rd person
Some character is or 3stones*

28

The 'Busacca'

It's not always that children—at once sworn enemies and friends of animals—have within their reach so rich and varied a store of natural wealth as was to be found in the zoos of the big cities before the bombs had set free rattlesnakes and tropical animals. There are—the more so in countries still called civilised—children almost completely deprived of the fabulous bestiary of one's infancy, children for whom the Pillars of Hercules are represented by the dog, the cat and the horse, and even these not always the best specimens. In these circumstances the boys of my generation, who knew practically nothing about the game of football or about any other game, used to rely for their amusement on their imagination, and on the legends of olden times. If the menagerie was missing, it was not beyond them to invent one for themselves—each, of course, after his own fashion. A child whom I used to know well, and whom everybody called Zebrino because of the striped jersey he usually wore (and even in the choice of the nickname there was perhaps a certain inkling as to his future inclinations and tastes), had to grow up in a place almost devoid of zoological interest, with the result that he had to draw upon ancient lore and folk tales, which he turned to good account. He used to spend his summer holidays by the sea shore, cut off from the rest of the world by great walls of rock. There were no usable roads around. The train used to wind its way through the tunnels, naturally without stopping, only a few rumblings and wisps of smoke suggesting it had passed at all. It was a kind of landing-stage, almost devoid of vegetation, where only yew-trees, squirrels and birds could find any kind of permanent home. But it was not wolf or wild boar country—they need heaths and forests. Zebrino, not yet a hunter himself, seldom accompanied those who did go out hunting. The various kinds of birds of passage were nothing but names to him, and didn't really excite his imagination.

But with the local birds—the goatsucker, the 'busacca', for example—he had, from the very outset, formed a close friendship. That he had ever actually seen one of them alive was rather doubtful—but at least once he had seen a dead goatsucker with its hairy, beakless and sucking mouth, even though in these parts goats were a rarity. But the 'busacca'? Even its very existence had been questioned by people more knowledgeable and experienced than Zebrino. None of the hunters Zebrino had ever met could boast of having killed one. It was, or at least it was supposed to be, a bird of prey, bigger than a hawk but smaller than an eagle, with wings strong enough but not large enough to enable it to rise vertically from the ground. When surprised by a hunter it would throw itself from the top of a rock, remaining balanced in the air like a glider or a kite, before landing again farther up or farther down, according to the wind and its own daring, but always somewhere it could dive off from again. An elusive demon, cunning and cumbersome, tough as leather and bullet-proof. Dead hawks and kestrels, black hoopoes and woodpeckers, would sometimes emerge, crumpled and limp as dirty handkerchiefs, from the pockets of poachers; but never a 'busacca'; it was an unattainable dream.

It was this dream that turned Zebrino into a one-day hunter. He had no gun and at his age there was no question of getting a shooting licence. And yet Zebrino, who had great compassion for dead birds and no intention of following in the footsteps of Saint Uberto, proudly set himself a task no one had ever achieved; bagging a busacca on his first day, after which he would give up shooting forever. Restin, the son of one of his *métayers*, just as young and weaponless as Zebrino, but better informed about guns, offered his help. Working together for some days, they got hold of a lead tube, which they attached to a piece of wood shaped like a rifle butt. At the point of interjection they made a hole for a fuse. They loaded the gun with black powder from the mines, squashed a handful of small square pieces of lead, cut out with scissors, into the charge, and then—in order to close both the charge and the leads—they thrust paper into the tube, ramming it home with a stick. There could only be one shot, so at no cost must it misfire. Eventually they set out one day before dawn, equipped with matches and a fuse stolen from the local miners.

One had to get very close to the 'busacca', lighting the match first and then, at the first signs of the bird's alarm, the fuse. Next, with the gun pointed towards it, for ten or twenty seconds, it had to be stalked, until the shot went off . . . it was then simply a question of watching it fall. The job of aiming the shot Zebrino reserved for himself. Restin's task was to decide when to light the fuse. The division of labour was exact and the honours would be evenly divided.

They walked for two or three hours, leaving behind them the last of the orchards and the sparse olive groves, entering the pine area, and then climbing the high cockpit of rocks overlooking the nearby valleys. The sea glinted in the distance and from the stone quarries they could hear occasional sounds of hammering.

The miraculous encounter took place sooner than expected—a vast shadow skimmed the surface of the water, squeezing itself into a crevice high up the cliff face and dispersing a whole flock of agitated birds.

— It's the busacca — Zebrino cried out, convinced that there could be only one 'busacca' and that this was it.

— Are you sure? — Restin was trembling with emotion.

— Quite sure. I'm going to aim. Get ready. Light the first match. — They tiptoed towards the spot. Restin lighted a first, then a second and finally a third match, wrinkling his nose at the smell of the burning sulphur. He stood by Zebrino like his own shadow, almost at the rock edge. There was a sudden crash, followed by a hissing. The trees shook as if some huge object had brushed them. Restin held the last match to the fuse.

— Yes . . . yes — Zebrino said, offering him the arm which was now in its firing position. It was only a question of a second,

31

but it seemed like an eternity. The smoke curled up into the air. At this moment they saw a common bird—perhaps a sparrow or a greenfinch—rise off the rock and settle on the bare branch of an umbrella pine. The explosion would take place any time. Zebrino hadn't the courage to look round, and almost without meaning to, aimed the gun at the creature and fired. The gun was flung from his hands and fell, shattered, to the ground. Clouds of smoke enveloped them, the echo reverberating through the valleys. — Are you hurt? — Restin, white as a sheet, asked Zebrino anxiously.

— No, but it's been a close shave — Zebrino mumbled gazing at the bits of gun at his feet.

The greenfinch had not moved from its branch and was chirruping curiously at them.

They heard the sound of footsteps. A miner, with an old Alpine hat, and a Franciscan friar were leaping down the rocks. They were on their way into the town, having been summoned there by the police. When Restin told them about the busacca (Zebrino, disapproving, kept making angry gestures, asking him to keep quiet), the miner made no comment, but simply pointed to the distant horizon.

— The 'busacca' . . . eh the 'busacca' — he said, suggesting it belonged to other climes.

He took a tin of meat from his pocket, wanting to share it with the two boys and the priest. Then all four of them went down in silence towards the silver of the olive-trees.

childhood adventure
failure but nothing is lost

Laguzzi and C.

Between Mrs. L., who lived in a flat above ours in Via Asmara, and my mother, there wasn't, to be sure, much love lost. So that whenever some article of clothing that she had spread out for drying, fell on our balcony, our neighbour did not think it proper to come and collect it, or to entrust the job to some reliable person. Instead she would lean out of the window with a long rod and elastic hook—a kind of fishing rod—and a line of cord dangling from it, and thus armed she would start an operation which after numerous attempts would eventually end up with the recovery of the object. I was a child and not particularly fond of the life of the sea, although I used to spend at least three months every year at the seaside. Hence this form of fishing so obstinately indulged in by Mrs. Laguzzi became permanently impressed on my child's imagination, so that I have never been able to see a fishing-hook without its conjuring up a vision of handkerchiefs, petticoats, or bras. More honest than Shakespeare's Autolycus, who used to haul up other people's clothing from hedges, the good Signora Laguzzi made use of her hook only for the recovery of her own clothing, an activity to which she was perfectly entitled. Except, of course, in the eyes of the child (myself) who made every effort to see that the prey should not fall into her clutches.

It was a large balcony and had two sides. Only my father used to stroll there after dinner. In the mornings, at about eight o'clock or so, I used to hang about waiting for the coach to pick me up and take me to school with the other more fortunate children. Corso Asmara was a steep winding street in the outskirts of the town, and so it was not much frequented. In other words, it was not a particularly high class area. However, looking from the terrace, one could see the house belonging to an aristocratic family, which owned carriages and horses and used to have footmen in livery. They were well known and generally respected. Theirs was a world that seemed quite inaccessible to me, even at my most optimistic. The only person I knew in Corso Asmara was a tobacconist from whom I used to buy the Cavour cigars that were my father's favourite and sweets for myself. And the only other people I could possibly meet there were the tremulous 'barba I' ('uncle I') so-called because of the prolonged ih! ih! he was in the habit of uttering every now and then while driving his ice-cream hand-cart—and Pippo Bixio, my childhood enemy, who sometimes beat me up and robbed me of my cigars and sweets.

After a few years, we moved house and went to live in another part of the town. It was a modern flat, with little light, but plenty of compensations—a lift, a radiator (always turned off), and a dining-room shaped like a dogfish. By the time I had finished school I was eighteen, then soon twenty and I started going out. I used to walk aimlessly under the arcades, since I had neither friends nor acquaintances. But I never went through Corso Asmara again. One day a sculptor, whom I'd met by chance, decided to take me under his wing, announcing that I had an 'interesting' temperament and promising to introduce me around. He kept his word turning up at the meeting place in bowler hat and patent leather shoes. Within half an hour our hired carriage had deposited us at the fortress I used to watch from the balcony of my old home. It was like a dream come true.

I was introduced to the mistress of the house, one of his relatives and the German governess—all big fat women whose hands the sculptor kissed. And then their fair-haired children appeared—two boys and a girl—all of whom seemed on excellent terms with the sculptor. It seemed to me an elegant house, with all kinds of water-colours and other paintings on the walls, much admired by everyone for their apparent modernity. We went round the garden overlooking the port below, an incomparably charming view. Tea was served from the *samovar*, a polished but ramshackle contraption. Everyone spoke fluent Italian, though with pronounced accents. A discussion took place about an article on Fogazzaro's *Leila* that appeared in *Caffaro*, and a white-haired gentleman present sang *Zazà, piccola zingara*, in which he was joined by the governess.

I spent a couple of hours there, which on account of my shyness seemed an eternity, and then got up to go. I was told, almost in a whisper, that they hoped I would come again. I was accompanied by the younger son Giacinto, the enviable sculptor staying on for dinner. Giacinto, who was about my age was kind enough to accompany me some of the way towards Corso Asmara. In this manner we reached my childhood balcony. Here, while Giacinto shook hands somewhat patronisingly, I looked up and saw, or saw again, with a tug at my heart Signora Laguzzi's fishing-rod hanging from the window. No doubt the indomitable old woman had quarrelled with our successors too. It would only have been a matter of a few seconds, but, since neither Giacinto and his family, nor the sculptor, knew anything about my past, I had no great urge to tell them. I asked him abruptly:

— What on earth do they do here? Do they fish?

— It looks like it — remarked Giacinto distractedly. — I sometimes see this fishing-rod as I go by. God knows what it's meant for . . . It's a rather lower middle-class sort of establishment, you know.

The thrust had gone home but I received it unblinkingly. Only Pippo Bixio, that thief, could have given me away, had we run into him. But this dreaded meeting never took place— neither then nor at any other time. And it really was the beginning of a new life for me.

1st person,

Escape from poverty

The House with the Two Palm-trees

The train was about to pull in. At every momentary glimpse between one tunnel and another—which looked like an instant or an eternity according as to whether the train was a fast or a slow one—the villa appeared and disappeared. It was a yellowish, somewhat dull-coloured pagoda, and one could have a side view of it from the train, as well as of the two palm-trees in front of it, which were symmetrical but not identical. They were planted as twins in the year of grace 1900. But the one grew faster and soon out-topped the other. There was no way of checking its growth or accelerating that of the other. That day it was a slow train and so, although half-hidden by more recent constructions, the villa had long been visible. On the western side, at the top of a small flight of stairs and hidden by a pittosporum hedge, someone (mother, aunt, cousin or nephew) used to stand and wave a handkerchief or a towel in order to greet whoever happened to be arriving, and above all to rush (if the person responded by waving back) to put the 'gnocchi' in the pot. The guest in question would then arrive, duly tired and hungry, within six or seven minutes. Five hours of train and smoke!

That day there was no one to wave the white handkerchief from the top of the stairs, which made Federigo feel dismal. He withdrew his head inside as the train entered the last tunnel . . . and started getting ready to leave by removing his suitcase from the rack, and resting his fingers on the door-handle. The engine slowed down with a long hissing sound, the light came back, and the train stopped with a big jerk. Federigo got down and with a certain effort pulled his heavy suitcase to the ground. It was a small station in between the openings of two tunnels and right in front of a steep slope of rocks and vineyards. Those who

remained on the train soon disappeared in the dark again.
— Porter? — asked a barefoot, sunburnt man, drawing near
the only traveller with a collar and tie.
— Here it is — said Federigo as he handed over his suitcase
to the porter and wondered who he could be, since his face
seemed familiar. Then with a sudden flash of realisation he
added in a warm voice:
— And so, Gresta, how is everything with you? — and
hastened to shake hands with him.

Gresta was a childhood friend of Federigo's, a hunting and
fishing companion whom Federigo had not seen for the last
thirty years and had quite forgotten over the last twenty. A
native of this place, and born of a peasant family, Gresta
had the advantage of mixing with the children of the only
true gentility of the place, when Federigo was—or thought
he was—the son of a gentleman. They climbed down the
stairs, which brought them right to the sea, with only a low
wall and a thin row of tamarisks standing between them and
the waves. To the left of those who descended these stairs
there was another invisible tunnel leading to the village; and
to the right, a few houses of the ex-emigrants perched on the
top of rocks scattered here and there and surrounded by poorly
cultivated gardens. One had to follow that way and then
turn right into a dry valley before getting to the pagoda from
which no one—no, not even a single person—had waved a
white handkerchief. They kept talking as they walked. Federigo
seemed to have rediscovered in himself a dialect he thought he
had altogether forgotten. And since Gresta—so-called because
of a crest of hair on his head, of which now there was no
trace left—had remained just the same in all respects, and
since the path and the houses too had remained just the same,
that escape from what had now become his habitual world,
that recovery of a time that had seemed almost unreal, had
something quite miraculous about it. For a moment Federigo
thought he had just gone mad and he seemed to have an
intuition of what it would be like were one's past to be 'played

back over and over again' in a *ne varietur* edition, from beginning to end just like a record cut once and for all.

But if one came to think of it, there were, of course, certain variants (for instance, the absence of the handkerchief waved as a sign of greeting), and consequently Federigo's sense of bewilderment was short-lived. Gresta, however, was quite unaware of all this. He kept talking of the sardine-fishing, the harvest, the first passage of the wood-pigeons and incidentally also of the passage of the German troops and the amount of vexation it caused. But even here the blending of the old and the new was not meant to convince Federigo of the validity of his first impression regarding the reversibility of the temporal order.

A potassium-coloured house, with something resembling a bungalow standing on the second floor, seemed, however, to clinch the first impression; for every stone, every patch of land and even the smell of rotten fish and the tar all around the house dragged Federigo perilously down into the well of memories. But here again Gresta promptly came to his aid and saved him from a certain embarrassment by telling him that Signor Grazzini, the barefoot and corpulent owner of this house, who had made a large fortune by swallowing diamonds in the mines of South Africa, had died quite some time ago, and that his property had passed into other hands. Then just a couple of steps off and there was a house to let, painted in a colour like that of blood-pudding, from which Federigo was fearfully waiting to see the no less corpulent figure of Signor Cardelli emerge. Signor Cardelli enjoyed a fairly high reputation in the village even though he had killed his wife by kicking her in the belly. But this fear did not come true either, because there was not a single trace left of the Cardelli family anywhere around.

But what about the lawyer Lamponi, who had induced his younger brother to commit suicide in order to get the money on his insurance policy? (A bottle-green turreted chalet.) And Cavalier Frissi who had more than once set fire to his empty shop in Montevideo and thus amassed a fortune? (A monstrous fabric of towers, little columns, intertwined serpents and creepers that attracted a huge swarm of insects and mice into the house. And from within the house the infernal din of an old-fashioned gramophone emitting songs like *Ridi pagliaccio*, *Niun mi tema*, *Chi mi frena in tal momento?*—and *Caramba*, the impetuous exclamations of an old choleric drunkard.)

For a few moments it appeared to the anxious Federigo as if he might run into the two neighbours living in that area: one in shorts, with his belly protruding on to his bare thighs and a gold chain dangling on his hairy chest; the other with a sulky face and a straw *sombrero*, surrounded by women in mourning and by the thick and tangible halo of the 'position' attained as well as of the charity generously bestowed. But there was no such risk. Gresta mentioned other names and other owners. It was only the houses with their plaster coming off and the sails of a windmill that carried Federigo back to the days of his youth.

And finally there was that narrow gorge at the end: the dry ditch with a little path overhead, the red bridge, the rusty gate and the avenue leading up to the pagoda hidden behind the two palm-trees. The gravel crunched under Federigo's shoes. There was a titmouse hanging from the bough of a fig-tree and making the air resound with its vocal arabesque. From the washerwomen's puddle a white-haired, though not old, woman stepped out to greet Federigo.

Federigo said no more than 'Oh Maria' and it seemed as if time had slid back some thirty years and Federigo returned to his own old self, without, however, losing his hold on the riches he had subsequently acquired. But what kind of riches? There were no diamonds, no shops burnt, no relatives dispatched to the land of the forefathers, no material and utilitarian contact with the local *goods*. An assiduous and involuntary process of extirpation, a long circumnavigation through modes and ideas of life quite unknown here, and the immersion in a time not marked by Signor Frissi's sun-dial. This—or a little more—was all the wealth he had got. And yet the suitcase was heavy.

At the bottom of the staircase Federigo took leave of Gresta, giving him a tip and a warm handshake, and followed the girl, now grown old, who had spent all her life in Federigo's family. They chatted informally, without, however, mentioning how old they had both become. They talked of the living, but even more of the dead, as they arrived in front of the pagoda. Federigo looked round and recognised the vast amphitheatre with the sea almost breaking into it, and the poplar leaning towards the greenhouse where he had shot his first bird with the Flobert. He raised his glance towards the windows of the third floor where his ancestors' portraits were hanging and then visited the dining-room on the ground-floor where he could not help noticing that from the wrinkled walls the panoply of spears and arrows had disappeared—a present from a junior signal-station officer who had spent a long time in Eritrea. But the woodcut of a young and solemn Verdi was still there. Federigo hastily went through the apartment and when he re-read the trademark 'The Preferable Sanitary Closet' written at the base of a certain porcelain seat, he felt his heart sinking as if he had encountered a family ghost. For these were the very first English words he had learnt. In that closet everything had remained just the same. But elsewhere he noted certain differences: additional beds, empty cradles, new sacred pictures stuck to the mirrors—signs of other lives that had replaced his own. Then he went to see the kitchen where Maria was blowing on the coals, and spread a mosquito-net over what was going to be his bed. And finally he stretched himself on a deck-chair in front of the house, of which only the fifteenth portion still belonged to him.

Federigo said to himself: a few days' holiday in the company of my dead people; they would pass quickly. But then all of a sudden he apprehensively reminded himself of the flavour of the food that he was going to get here. Not that it was bad, but it was *that* particular flavour—a family flavour transmitted from generation to generation which no cook could ever destroy. A continuity this, which even if destroyed elsewhere, endures through the grease of the sauce, the strong garlic smell, the smell of onions and basil, the stuffing pounded in the marble mortar. Attracted by this smell even the dead, condemned to a much lighter food, return to the earth from time to time.

'But haven't you got a house of your own on the sea?' his friends would ask him if they met him by chance on some fashionable beach where even the sea seems to be served in tin-pots. Of course, he *did* have such a house—or at least the fifteenth part of it—and he came back precisely to revisit it.

A soft tinkling sound of the glass from within the house announced that dinner was ready. The sea-horn his brother used to blow like a Roman trumpet for rallying the family was no longer there. What had become of it? Surely he would have to look for it.

Federigo got up, aimed his finger at the titmouse that had had the cheek to follow him and come as close as the poplar by the greenhouse, and fired a mental shot.

— How silly I am! — he stammered — I am going to enjoy my stay.

The Bearded Woman

The elderly man in an elegant grey suit, standing by the gate of the Collegio dei Barnabiti and watching the pupils come out, hadn't at first attracted any attention from the few grown ups who were also waiting there. Only the porter muttered 'I've never seen him before. What can he be up to?' The children came out in twos and threes and sometimes alone. Very few found anyone waiting to take them home. But among those present, the elderly man, much to his disappointment, didn't see any maidservant. A couple of maids with hats on, yes—but no maidservant.

The elderly man—let us call him M.—murmured: 'I'm not surprised,' and walked slowly away towards the arcades of Via XX Settembre. The arcades were much the same as they had been forty years ago and the school building itself hadn't changed much. Signor M., on the other hand, had changed a great deal and he knew it. But since he avoided looking at his own reflection in shop windows, he managed to persuade himself that the past forty years hadn't touched him at all. As a result he stretched out his hand towards the woman who approached him, handed her his lunch box, as well as the packet of books wrapped up in oilcloth secured by a rubber band, and let himself be led towards the steep stretch of road running into Via Ugo Foscolo. This part of the road was particularly crowded, its heavy traffic of cars and trucks seldom paying much attention to the *bacchifero*—the man with the stick, as the constable used to be called in the town. Then, at the foot of the deserted twisting street named after the singer of 'Le Grazie', Signor M. dropped the old woman's hand and set off on his own. She followed him, slow and stooping, clutching the lunch box and books in her shaky hands. The distance between the two widened gradually until she was unable to keep pace with 'the rogue'.

Signor M. knew perfectly well that he was no longer a

'rogue' and that the woman Maria had died some thirty years ago in an old people's home. She had been put there at their own expense, as it was no longer possible to keep the decrepit eighty-year-old woman at home. All this he knew —but since the streets and the houses between the elementary school and his home of forty years ago were almost the same, he didn't find it all that strange that he should evoke, in detail, the woman who had guided his infant steps. It was because of this that he had stopped at the gate of that particular elementary school, since these were the only two places left where he could possibly evoke Maria—the route between the school and his parental home, and the kitchen of the house at Montecorvo where he hadn't set foot in years. In other houses, either demolished or long since in the hands of new tenants, such a thing was out of the question.

Prematurely old ever since the day she was born, illiterate, bent and bearded, Maria had been, for as long as anyone could remember, the faithful custodian of M.'s family fortunes —even before Signor M.'s father had married, and had a family. From her fifteenth to her eightieth year, Maria had been the guardian and manager of her adopted home. Of course, she had her own home too, but she visited it only when the family was spending the summer at Montecorvo. Moreover, she had to face a ten-hour walk in order to get there. In the early days she had undertaken this journey a number of times, but when she realised that people over there no longer remembered her or that they regarded her as a foreigner or an intruder, Maria had severed all ties with her ancestral home. She used to have two houses which were almost her own, one in the town and one in the country. She also had children, almost like her own, whom she used to take to school—children evenly spaced between the ages of two and fifteen, who required many years of devotion, providing at intervals a consoling repetition of the whole process. The pleasure of living comes from the repetition of certain acts and habits, and from the fact that one can say to oneself: 'I shall repeat everything

I've done and it will be more or less the same, but not exactly the same.' The pleasure derives from the element of diversity in what seems identical, and it's the same for an intellectual as for an illiterate person.

'Here she comes,' said Signor M., catching sight of her and hurrying towards Via Serra, panting up the Salita dei Cappuccini. At the top there was a dairy where he used to stop for a glass of milk and a couple of biscuits. This time, too, he stopped at the same place, but to his dismay found himself seated in a modern café, smelling of bitter *espresso* rather than of fresh milk. For a moment he felt at a loss, but when the waiter came he merely said 'Sorry' and walked out, to the surprise of the few people sitting there.

Maria arrived rather out of breath and for some minutes he walked beside her, teasing her at first playfully and then ironically. When she was only a child Napoleon's troops had passed through the Val di Levanto and Signor M. wanted to know how she had managed to protect herself. Wasn't the chastity she had been boasting of all her life merely a myth?

Even though Maria was born at least half a century after the passing of Napoleon's troops, she made up all sorts of implausible excuses. She kept saying that she remembered nothing—neither the soldiers nor their officers. No doubt she had had a fiancé, but she had never let him so much as touch her. He had gone away to find work and had never been heard of since. For all she knew, he might have been dead all these years.

Signor M. was reluctant to pursue a topic that seemed to him incompatible with the ten-year-old he had become in his mind's eye. And yet there was nothing else to talk about. Having gone back to his early childhood, he found that he couldn't get rid of that part of himself which had developed later. He saw Maria again at the old people's home. Virtually crippled by now, she still managed to keep in touch with those around her and with the nuns, who were particularly stingy

when it came to things like sugar. He re-read the announcement of her death many years after he had left his parents'
home. Where was the old woman buried? Who could possibly
know? He had never visited her grave; had even forgotten
Maria except that at odd, unhappy moments in his life, her
image would return. Signor M. was possibly the only person
in the world who had the faintest memory of her. At times he
had struggled with that memory, trying to get rid of it as one
would old clothes. In each house where a family has lived
for many years, there is a jug or some useless trifle that no
newcomer can ever tamper with. In the life of Signor M.,
who no longer had a home, there was no such object. The
only thing left for him was that flickering, breathless shadow
he had tried for years to shake off but which still accompanied
him, panting in her effort to keep pace with him.

A futile life? Surely it would be a mistake to think so, Signor
M. reflected. When all the old servants are dead; when all the
particles of the universe have a name, an identity and a function;
when the perfect balance is struck between the rights and
responsibilities of everyone, who of us can walk home with a
ghost and banish the horror of loneliness by feeling at his side
the protective presence of an angelic and bearded spirit?

Signor M. was leaning over the parapet as he looked down
at the vast stretch of the grey roof-tops, the port, the *Laterna*,
and far beyond the sluice gates and the wind-lashed sea.
One could reach it by lift from the heart of the city. From
time to time the box-like object appeared and people hurried
out of it, disappearing into the Piazza without even noticing
that all too familiar view.

Signor M. was surprised to hear a voice call him by name.
'Well, what a surprise! What on earth are you doing here? It
must be thirty years since we last met!'

It was an old school-friend—though not from the elementary
school—a man of Signor M.'s own age with nondescript
features. Signor M. tried to remember his name—Burlamacchi?
. . . Cacciapoti? . . . It must have been four syllables.

45

— Yes — he said — How nice to see you again. I am just passing through and stopped here for a little. . . .

Signor M. stammered. Suppose the man observed him? He turned round and saw several old women and children by the parapet. But they paid no attention to him. In any case there was no Maria among them. Either she had not yet arrived or she had gone ahead on her own.

— I'm in a hurry to get down — he said, moving towards the lift. — Good-bye. Hope to see you again sometime—I don't know. . . .

He took the lift, the doors closed and the cabin plunged rapidly downwards. The other man went his way through the Circonvallazione, shaking his head.

In the Key of 'Fa'

You should start from this *re* and then close, bringing the voice in *'maschera'* — the old *maestro* explained, tapping on the keyboard. — Later, you can even open the *mi* B flat, if necessary, but for the time being . . . say *u*. Yes, that's it: *O-o-o-uuu* . . . Very good.

I seemed to be uttering an unearthly groan, an inhuman hissing sound; but the old *maestro* was satisfied. Small, doubled over the keyboard, venerable and at the same time ridiculous, he used to modulate the notes with his mouth formed like a pigeon's egg, a mouth that had some difficulty in opening from its tufted surrounds of moustache and the tremulous slopes of snow-white beard. He would trill like an ancient nightingale with his little eyes twinkling behind thick lenses.

The windows (we were on the top floor of the house) opened on to a large square with huge umbrellas and market stalls scattered over it. One could see in the distance the statue of an Argentine general on an eternally prancing bronze horse, heroically brandishing his sabre in the air. The avenue to the right, leading to the sea, was very quiet and one could read the name-plates of washer-women and obscure dentists.

The *maestro* used to live rather off the beaten track, but I had to put up with that. For he alone, he who had worked with Maurel and Navarrini, and had received such applause that the *Imperiale* of Pietrasanta and the *Liceo* of Barcellona had practically collapsed, might have saved me from the ghastly incompetence of the Conservatorio teachers.

The lessons used to start very early, that's to say at half-past eight in the morning, and would normally last half an hour. From there I used to go to the Biblioteca Comunale, as a rule deserted at that hour. There wasn't much to choose from among the books and the assistant obviously didn't like being disturbed. But on a particular shelf that was always open I found material to last me for months. (It was there that I

47

happened to read I don't know how many books by Lemaître and Scherer.) In the meantime my lessons continued. I was gradually resigning myself to having to relinquish what had been, so to speak, my psychological voice. No more Boris, no more Gurnemanz, no more Filippo II; I would have to forget the notes under the lines, the sepulchral sounds of the eunuch Osmin and of Sarastro. The old *maestro* was firm on this point; not even in the new register would he let me nourish too many hopes about my wearing one day Iago's plumed fez or Scarpia's monocle and snuff-box. He abhorred the 'modern', which, according to him, would have ruined me. The sort of music that he thought good for me was traditional *bel canto*: Carlo V, Valentino, Father Germont, Belcore the sergeant, Dr. Malatesta: this was what I needed.

'Giardini dell'alcazar—de'mauri Regi delizie—oh quanto....' *Do do do do* hammered again and again like a gong; then arabesques and ornamentations, going further and further up to an acute *fa* which reached the general's statue, then release into the *do* in the middle, with its irresistible effect. Like Alfonso XII, the king of Castiglia, the old *maestro* had won his battle forty years ago, when Don Pedro of Brasile had been seen rubbing the skin off his palms in appreciation. What a pity, though! I could no longer recognise my old voice nor appreciate the new one. I was in possession of an instrument that I had no use for. At the end of half an hour other pupils, whom I soon came to know, began to arrive. A bespectacled accountant from Lloyd Sabaudo, a police inspector (Mr. Calastrone), a scraggy woman, with short legs and a pagoda of artificial curls, the wife of an industrialist, who (she told me as soon as we met) did not understand her—all these followed me in the *Lombardi's* terzetto. One day, while sitting outside I spent some time listening to the din ('Qual voluttà trascorrere . . .') with which the irritated passers-by were being deluged.

Madame Poiret invited me to her house more than once. She used to live in an embattled and turreted villa accessible only over a draw-bridge. She came from Caravaggio, in spite of her husband's French name, and she used to address me with *voi* twenty years before that unfortunate expression was to become obligatory. She had made her début in *Cavalleria* at Pontremoli, and then disappeared. She lacked everything except voice. It was from her that I learned that the old *maestro*, who was always reserved with me, used to regard me as the only worthwhile pupil fate had granted him in fifteen years of teaching. I was quite confused. Perhaps they had all decided to make fun of me? I tactfully interrogated the old *maestro*, who dispelled my doubts. I had to accept the verdict: neither Signora Poiret, nor the tramways engineer, who, while shouting the part of Amonasro, used to make the astonished fishmongers raise their heads, nor the daughter of the superintendent of the lunatic asylum, dark Mignon and the voluminous and feline Princess of Eboli, nor the tremulous and affected Nemorino of the 'Sabaudo', nor even (in his case there was, of course, no question at all) the unfortunate Mr. Calastrone, were worthy of tying my shoelaces. The voice, the old *maestro* said, did not count at all. What was needed was the *axillo* (we used to talk in dialect), or some pepper under one's tail. In the 'Santa Medaglia' of Valentino, the adolescent hero with the hempen hair, if everything went well, I could have been taken in the death scene for a new Kaschmann.

After that conversation I went out as ashamed of myself as a dog. How strange that the gift of the *axillo* had fallen on a wretched bookworm like myself? And what use would it have been to me, if they had assigned me the less juicy parts of the lyric repertoire?

With or without pepper, it was the devil who turned up to put in a tail. One day, on my return from a brief holiday, I was told that the old *maestro* had suddenly died. I saw him lying on a single bed, dressed in a dark suit, his face draped with long silvery hair. He had shrunk into something minute. Diplomas, medals of the Tsar, wreaths of artificial flowers, and framed newspaper cuttings were to be seen all round the room. His favourite pupils took it in turn to keep watch by his dead body, uttering small rat-like yelps in 'maschera' (*mi mi mi*).

After the funeral I left the country and soon the Pilotta Barracks at Parma claimed me. As far as I was concerned, the *incanto*, if not the *canto*, was finished. I think the old *maestro* had taken away with him that sonorous phantom—his own vocal *alter ego*—which, almost without my noticing it, he had laboriously tried to discover and develop in me, perhaps in order to rediscover his own far-off youth. When, years later, I sat at the keyboard again, I noticed that the deep *mi* of the Grande Inquisitore and the contrabass *re* of the fat Osmin had returned to their proper place.

But what use were they to me now?

Success

The other evening in the theatre the head-claqueur must have fallen asleep. (The good but rather unpopular opera had been conducive to sleep, rendering the usual dosage of 'well done' or 'bravo' somewhat difficult to administer.) Only in this way can I explain how an air sung by the bass, with its two strofas left in suspense, was interrupted by untimely applause towards the end of the first strofa, that is to say at a point where no sonorous clause, no effect of the voice, could conceivably have justified the sudden clapping of hands. What had happened? The head-claqueur, on waking up, had given an untimely signal: that was all. People shouted 'shut up'; the melody was resumed; but by now the trick of the game had been exposed, so that when the real effect came and the bass decided to lower the pitch of his voice, no one could be persuaded by the discredited signals coming from a place that was now topographically suspect.

One has to make a lot of allowance for the claqueurs. I don't think they earn much; and where the public shows an unjustified indifference towards the champions of the lyric art, they perform a necessary task. An opera or a melodrama without applause does not warm the heart; it is not even entertainment. To hear without seeing, when the curtain is up, Radamès and Ramfis after the concerted bellowing of 'immenso Ftà' and not to want to scrutinise their bath-gowns and their turbans at close quarters is to miss half the pleasure of *Aïda*; not to back up with a grumble of consent the gargle emitted by Sparafucile when he runs away from Rigoletto after having proposed that mean business to him, is to be lacking in charity, in human solidarity, to say the least. Not that that mildly grating sound is difficult as a sound, but it is something more than a sound; it is the symbol of the diver's whole life. Anyone who has ever lived in rented rooms, in fourth-class hotels and pensions, may have heard thousands of similar, un-Dostoevskian, 'sounds from the subsoil'.

The other evening the applause took me back to the past. Once the claqueurs used to be recruited from among barbers. They did not take it on as a job, but out of enthusiasm; and there was no harm if through that enthusiasm they could also make some money. I myself, when I decided to study singing, had my first introduction to the 'ambiente' from my barber. The barber Pecchioli, head-claqueur of my home town, was a real connoisseur; he rarely gave his signal, which consisted of snapping his forefinger against his thumb. With the better-known pieces, or after melodies producing more obvious effects, he allowed his initiates to do it, in the same way as the paying public. He would intervene only in doubtful cases; after some *pianissimo*, some rare *diminuendo*, or the most daring lowering of pitch. Then he would just whisper 'bravo' in so spontaneous a way that no one could possibly suspect that there was a fee for it.

For my part, I must confess I was not at the outset one of his favourite customers, being one of those who have recourse to the barber only for a hair-cut, and who decline the shampooing, the lotions, and the expensive massages which endear one to a barber. Nevertheless, on one occasion, he decided to enlist my temporary help, with the result that one evening I found myself in the company of his claqueurs. It was a novel, rather awkward occasion. A townsman of mine, just returned from Argentina, was giving a concert of his own work. José Rebillo, a pointillist painter and author of various kinds of music, was not, in the true sense, a musician at all. It was rumoured that he didn't even know the notes, but composed music directly on the pianola, clipping and punching rolls of cardboard with a pair of scissors and a drift. What came out of that contrivance was transcribed, harmonised and often orchestrated by others.

In those days modern music was represented almost exclusively by Wagner, whom most people had now come to tolerate. But music like Signor Rebillo's, all dissonance and screeching, had never been heard before. Was Rebillo a genius or a madman? Judging from the titles of his compositions —I remember, for instance, a 'Ninfea morente' presented like a 'musical still-life'—I would have had to conclude that he was at least a precursor. But I would have been even less capable of discerning it then than I am now.

So it happened that on the evening of the concert I too entered Politeama with a complimentary ticket and with the intention of discharging my duty. But just as the dying Nymph was breathing her last, and I was about to clap my hands, a chorus of hissing sounds and protests rose from all over the stalls and from every corner of the galleries. The hoarse sound of 'Viva Rebillo!' was drowned by an almost unanimous crying of *'Basta! fuori l'autore! fuori dalla porta!'* which turned into a diapason of *'Morte a Berillo!'*, the musician's name getting very poetically distorted. Was there a counter-claque at work? Or did Signor Rebillo have a lot of enemies in the town? I have never been able to discover. Infected by the uproar and being a long way from Pecchioli, I hastened to join the majority, meanly adding my own voice to the voices of those who were shouting *'Abasso! alla porta!'* The evening ended amidst whistling and laughter and I disappeared without being noticed by my 'boss'.

Months later, I was taken to the house of the musician whom I had once booed. He was living in a neo-Gothic tower accessible only over an almost unusable drawbridge. Rebillo spent his time punching cardboard paper and spraying vast pieces of canvas. He spoke a coastal dialect with a sprinkling of creole words. His reading was confined to *Prensa* and *Scena illustrata*. How on earth avant-garde ideas had ever entered his head remained a mystery. Big, fat, bald, moustached and ignorant, Rebillo was probably the most inspired man ever born.

In Paris, perhaps, twenty years later, he might have been taken seriously. But in that commercial and down-to-earth town of his there was nothing doing. However, Rebillo's

53

circle of friends did not include only scroungers and claqueurs—parasites who turn up only at meal times and when they want money. His best friend and confidant, for instance, was a postal employee, Armando Riccò, a diminutive, smooth-skinned man, who wore a monocle with a ribbon, and who used to write Parnassian sonnets by the thousand. According to Riccò, one couldn't possibly write a line of prose without disqualifying oneself as a poet. He had a predilection for choice expressions; he wouldn't say 'gli uomini', but 'li umani'; and yet he affected to despise D'Annunzio. To the end of a long life he remained equally arrogant and unpublished. He said he worked for posterity. At about midnight, when the barbers and other guests had left, Rebillo and Riccò stayed on alone. The pianola, with the aid of whistlings and sneezes, started up and Riccò began reciting his poems, his eyes half shut, and laying special stress on the diaereses.

On calm and peaceful nights the waves broke gently against the escarpment which protected Signor Rebillo's neo-Gothic tower, and I think they do so even now, although the tower is no longer there. After his death, I don't know what happened to the mountains of rolls that used to encumber his study. The disposal of the verses of Armando Riccò, who died unknown, was, of course, less of a problem.

From such encounters I have learnt a truth vouchsafed to few people: art bestows its consolations above all on the unsuccessful. That is why it plays such an important role in people's lives; and why the musician Rebillo and the poet Riccò, of whom I was unconsciously reminded the other evening by that awkward claqueur, perhaps deserved their memorial tribute.

Il lacerato spirito

I have seen, and in part heard, a collection of the old records of songs and piano music cut between 1903 and 1908. The old gentleman who initiated me into the secrets of his discoteca is the last custodian of the vocal relics of that period. Some forty years ago when he was young the death-knell for the *bel canto* had already been tolled and there were no such things as records in what was considered to be the golden age of the *bel canto*. But when the new invention made it possible to imprison the heroic voices that were still there in a box (the earliest wax gramophones really *did* look like tins of preserved tomatoes), its technical inadequacies could embalm ghost voices, nothing more. So that what issued from this instrument was a series of strident and disembodied voices, which had an altogether different timbre. And the deeper the voices, the more unrecognisable they were. Today only an initiate can critically 'reconstruct' the invocation of the *Ebrea* 'Se oppressi ognor . . .' as it was sung at the beginning of this century by the gigantic Navarrini (well over six foot tall), the burden of age and glory on his shoulders.

The famous artists of those times—and they were right—did not approve of the new invention. Faced with the prospect of appearing before posterity in such a bogus manner, they preferred to be forgotten rather than be heard in this way. But later one of them gave in; and then another. In 1903, during the première at the New York Metropolitan, it was possible to hide in the wings and catch a glimpse of Vasco de Gama's embarkation and hear the song 'O paradiso' it inspired, sung by the tenor De Reszke, including even the background music and the public ovations. The record was then cut in the usual fashion, edited and reproduced.

What I heard is considered to be the only copy left, and it is of immense value, like an antique. Anyone who knows by heart that passage of Meyerbeer with its endless subtleties would be able to make some sense of it; to others, however, it can only seem a mere buzzing interrupted by screeches, and finally drowned by a wave of shouts and applause that sound like insults. Nothing else remains of Jean de Reszke, and even the old man has never heard of any other recording.

It must have been a few years later that the aria 'Io non son che una povera ancella . . .' (Adriana Lecouvreur), sung by the great Angelica Pandolfini, who improvised her part, and *Don Giovanni's* daring serenade 'De' vieni alla finestra' sung by Victor Maurel, were recorded. Despite a thick layer of rust one can still be impressed by Angelica's performance. On the other hand, the arbitrariness and vulgarity of the singer who was, in France, the penultimate survivor of the Italian *bel canto*, are utterly stupifying. The yelps of *Home, sweet home*, produced by the then sixty-year-old Adelina Patti, are totally undecipherable, but elements of greatness still survive in the death of Tamagno's Othello (a Tamagno that has the voice of a gipsy). The concert was a long one; but I was more anxious to know the secret in the old man's keeping than to try to interpret the meaning of voices long since petrified. And before taking leave, I did indeed manage to get him to explain.

Being passionately enamoured of the art of singing, and being, like Leoncavallo's clown, at a loss to choose between theatre and life, at once shy and hard to please, proud and timid—he had spent the best part of his days trying in vain to achieve a perfect rendering of Jacopo Fiesco's celebrated aria *Simon Boccanegra*. Every day, from the age of eighteen to the age of fifty, standing before the mirror, his face covered with soap, shaving brush and razor put aside, he would move a few steps backwards; then, threatening the closed doors of the marble palace in front of the Duomo of San Lorenzo at Genoa with his fists, he would thunder forth 'A te l'estremo addio, palagio altero!' softening his voice for 'Il lacerato spirito del mesto genitore . . .', and finally lowering it as far as he could for 'Prega Maria per me . . .'.

It is not a difficult aria, but it requires an extremely mature voice and, when he was young, the old man felt that his voice was not mature enough. An inexperienced bass is like a raw, inedible fruit. The years sped by. Innumerable houses, barracks, hotels, boarding houses, clinics, hospitals and rented rooms resounded with the thundering invective. The voice, because still loose, kept maturing, until it began to lose first the *funnel* (or *tuba* as it is called), and one fine day, even its tone and resonance. The old man (who was not so old then) realised that the only thing for him to do was to take time by the fore-lock, grab at the perfection to which he aspired, and impress everybody with the famous aria. He could then sink into dignified silence. A medical friend of his, who had given up a brilliant career, often came to see him to try out the duet of the Puritani 'Suoni la tromba', but more often than not to attempt all by himself, with his eyebrows puckered and one finger on the piano, the sheriff Rance's bitter and sneering confession 'Minnie dalla mia casa son partito . . .' and its explosive conclusion 'Or per un bacio tuo getto un tesoro!' which had the unfortunate effect of provoking the wrath of both the porter and the neighbours. The former doctor had also been waiting for years for his voice to mature so that he could make his début. Alas, one morning he lost all patience, a thin harsh voice issued from his throat, and the aspirant sheriff jumped out of the window, nailing himself on the spikes of a railing in the garden below. He died instantaneously, without suffering.

The future collector of records took a hint from this, abandoning reluctantly his own efforts after perfection. He was now fifty; and the moment he had been waiting for all these years passed unnoticed, least of all by himself. Except that from time to time, while shaving, he still moves a few steps backward to intone in a tremulous voice, 'Il lacerato spirito . . .'. Always, at that very moment, the ghost of his old friend appears beside him and his voice dries up on his lips. Moreover, for whom can he sing today? The art of singing is in complete decline.

The Ostrich Feather

Men are more or less like books: you read one of them absent-mindedly, without realising that it will leave an indelible mark. You devote to another all the attention it seems to deserve, only to find a few months later that it's all been a complete waste of time. But at the very first contact, the ultimate result—whether positive or negative—is hanging in the balance. I often ask myself, not which books, but which men among the living or the dead, I should like to have another glimpse of if, God forbid, I were to stand before a firing squad or were going to be drowned. Men or favourite animals? Men—or women—who were dear to me or men I had met only casually and known only superficially, and who would never have suspected that they could occupy such a place in my heart.

If one could compare those moments which precede sleep and which ought to be spent in prayer and meditation with the last moments of one's life, I would say that there would be many a surprise in store for the *homo sapiens* of our times, who lives in a society where the more concern one shows for the rights of the community, the more inhuman it all seems.

The other evening, before falling asleep, as I was trying to concentrate on the meaning of life and repeating to myself 'I am born to die', two strange figures whom I had quite forgotten came to visit me.

A gentle knock—toc, toc, toc—followed by a gruff, 'May I come in?' which implied at least an equally gruff *yes, of course* preceded the entry of a tough-looking soldier. Medium-sized and, like the ghost in *Hamlet*, armed from head to foot, he had, attached to his cap, an ostrich feather curving down almost as far as his spurs. At his side there stood a servile and ceremonious old man who expressed himself more through gestures and lemur-like grimaces than through any comprehensible dialect.

— Marcello — I said at once, thinking of the faithful servant

58

of Raoul de Nangy in *Ugonotti*. The thought of this character, inevitably associated with that of the famous actor made me recognise, beyond any doubt, the person who had died years ago in Montevideo and who had been the executor of the most sepulchral notes the Italian theatre has ever known: the deep bass Gaudio Mansueto, a broad-shouldered man, ex-*camallo* or unloader from the port of Genoa. When I came to know him, he had become, thanks to a successful career as a lyric artist, rather more polished; and in virtue of natural intelligence he could, when 'in parte', completely dominate the stage.

— Marcello — the soldier admitted, sharpening his already pointed moustache *alla Marco Praga* and, approaching the piano which was always open, he ran his hand over the keyboard and launched softly into the *pif paf* which introduces the description of the Roccella. The panes rattled. — Ah — I said, without showing any surprise. — And turning to the other — Excuse me, what about you? — To-night I dress like Dulcamara or Alcindoro, in order to serve you; my name is Astorre Pinti; comic bass, or buffoon, just as you please — Astorre Pinti? Of course I know you, Signor Astorre. We once had a long conversation hidden in a house in Via Lamarmora 14, during those infernal days before the liberation of Florence. — (Hairy, famished, always in pyjamas and with his chest loaded with trinkets and badges, his voice perpetually 'in maschera' — *mi mi mi* on three octaves, the squeak of a dormouse and then a death-rattle—he and his numerous family had gone without meals for days. And in his case the question was even more complicated. Was he alive or dead like the other fellow? I hadn't heard anything about him for ages.)

— Of course, Commendatore Mansueto — I resumed, trying to conceal my embarrassment — you wouldn't remember that I had the honour of being introduced to you thirty years ago by Pecchioli, the hairdresser in Galleria Mazzini. You took me with you to the piano tuner who was also the head of the *claque*, and heard me sing 'Lacerato spirito', and encouraged me to go on with my training.

59

— Ah, ah — Mansueto thundered, and Dulcamara grinned 'ah ah' in perfect unison.

They sat together at the piano and, taking no notice of me, started playing the harp. They picked up the score of *La forza del destino* from the shelf, going straight to the page they were looking for.

— I remember, Cavaliere Astorre — I added — your predicting the total destruction of Florence, the city of blasphemers; but of course you were only partly right. As for you, Commendatore, I was lucky enough to meet you again when you were dressed as Zaccaria on the stage of the Chiarella at Turin; but then I lost track of you.

— Ah, ah, ah — echoed Mansueto and Astorre followed up with the 'ah, ah, ah' of the two conspirators in *Ballo in maschera*.

— I can't flatter myself — I continued — that I will be remembered—modest hack as I am—by the authentic luminaries of the opera. Nevertheless, if your lordships would like to explain. . . .

— "Giudizi temerari" . . . — Marcello exploded, flinging his hat to the ground and starting his part in the duet of the two friars. A piece of broken feather flew over the piano. And the last syllable got choked, producing a deep sound like an organ, muffling the screeching of the late-night trams. From the room above someone thumped on the floor. No doubt the neighbours were already up.

— I congratulate you — I went on, putting my hands to my ears — I congratulate you, Commendatore, on the fact that in spite of your age, in spite of the changed conditions . . . of life and of . . . circumstance, the range of your voice has retained its pristine strength. However, considering the late hour and the habits of these fellow-tenants . . . would it not be inopportune . . . I hope you understand me . . . The world . . .

— 'Del mondo i disinganni' . . . — burst out Mansueto, twisting himself on the revolving chair and accompanying himself with the help of his own loud slaps, while the other supported him

60

with a low counter singing, derisive and biting in its effect, in the hope that his strident voice would make headway amidst such a din.

The storm had broken out in full. A tempest of high- and low-pitched voices, impudent monkish laughter and piping trills against a ravine: the lesson in humility from the Father Guardian and the doubts and bawdy jokes of Melitone. I tried to interrupt, but my voice was drowned. It lasted for some time before being finally extinguished by garrulous Astorre's vain attempt—two octaves further up—at counterpoint.

When I unblocked my ears, I heard somebody knocking hard on the outer door .The whole building was in an uproar. I could even hear loud voices and curses from the street.

— That's all — said the Commendatore as he shut the piano with a bang, and Astorre echoed 'That's all' as he picked up the bowler-hat he had thrown aside. The two men were now on their feet and bowing.

— Servitor — both broke out in the voice of Gounod's Mefisto, descending to a *fa diesis* which seemed to have come straight from hell, and then they left, apparently satisfied with the night's performance. I remained in a state of excitement for a long while. The protesting voices had subsided and the exit of the warrior and the manikin seemed to have provoked no further comments. That they might have ridden off on a broom seemed unlikely to me. I could sleep very little and kept repeating to myself 'Del mondo i disinganni . . .', trying to grasp the significance of their mysterious visit. Was it the rendezvous between a living man and a dead one that I had witnessed, or was it just two ghosts on their nocturnal round? And if the two knew nothing about me, how could they have found out my address? And if they were merely the product of my subconscious, why could it not have produced someone more important?

Then I reflected that there was after all some link between these two. Having met Marcello once I had hoped that one day I would be able to emulate his glory, to follow in his footsteps. And as far as Astorre was concerned, having shared his hunger thirty years ago, I was thankful that I had been spared the hazards of *his* life, although I had to face some which were even more humiliating. The two men were the beginning and the end of an arch, of a personal and private parable. And they continued to ignore him for whom alone their lives had had any real significance.

When I got up I rang my neighbour on the floor above to offer my apologies. He answered, drily, that he had heard nothing during the night. Later on, when I discreetly questioned the woman who comes to clean my room, she admitted that she had found a feather between the wall and the piano.

— A chicken or pigeon feather — she specified — not ostrich. Perhaps the wind had blown it in.

The Best Comes Last

As soon as they sat down, her quick decisive choice earned her a bow of consent from the young waiter who appeared with the menu.

— Consommé, a plain *paillard*, a baked apple, and a *manzanillo*.

— *Manzanillo?* What's that? — asked the man with her. — The *manzanillo* tree kills you if you sleep under it. Its shadow is lethal. But as a drink it's a hit: it's said to be an infusion of carobs. It gives me a light and rather pleasant sort of nausea. But one's not enough; you need it three or four times a day.

He raised his arm, pointing to the figures in a publicity poster: smiling, happy men and women with egg-coloured hair, in evening-dress, sprawling in the shade of a huge tree.

The man was intent on the menu, but couldn't make up his mind what to order. An elderly and better-shaved waiter came up with a wine list. — Chiaretto, Bardolino, Chianti? Tokai del Friuli? Clastidio? Paradiso di Valtellina? Or Inferno?

— We'll have the Paradiso. I won't have anything else for the moment, but you can serve the lady in the meantime.

The waiters left and the man went on studying the menu.

— Trout — she said quietly — Sole *à la meunière*. Eel *alla livornese*. No, I don't like that, makes me think of the slimy stream near my house, which used to wind among rocks and reeds so that it was impossible to get over it except here and there. But it had the best eels in the world. Small yellowish ones, difficult to see under the soapy scum on the surface of the water.

One had to wade into the middle to catch them and grope with one's hands, keeping the water back as long as one could with bits of slate from the bottom. If an eel appeared and there was a fork at hand one could almost always transfix it with one stab, and bring it bleeding to the surface and throw it still writhing on the bank. Without a fork though it was a complicated job, for the eel would slip away through one's fingers to reappear under a soap bubble and then disappear again.

— But did you eat it? — she asked, spreading mustard on her *paillard* which still had the striped marks of the grill.

— Three or four of us used to, smoking it on a fire made of straw and waste paper. It tasted of smoke and mud, and was quite delicious. But it was only our first course. Usually we had something more substantial already waiting for us: a *beccafico*. For two or three hours we would lie in wait under an old poplar, hidden behind a hedge. My friends had a catapult, while I had the use of a shotgun loaded with three or four microscopic pellets.

'We'd see the honey-coloured bird hopping about on the fig tree, eating the fruit by opening it with rapid lunges of its thin, delicate beak. It seldom moved from the fig to the poplar, and it was impossible to hide under the fig. Nevertheless, two or three times during the season it happened that the *beccafico* (for it was always the same one) flew quickly across and perched on the poplar. It was either too high or too hidden in the branches and there was nothing one could do. Sometimes, though, on rare occasions, it landed lower, a yard or so off. Then all of us let fly together.

Our delicious meal could now start. Those were great occasions. We used to eat like that once or twice a year . . .'

— And what about drinks? — she asked, casually throwing back a large quantity of Manzanillo.

— A pail of water from the well, drawn up through ferns and plaster, with ten or twelve lemons—each as big as a walnut—squeezed into it.

The man remained silent for a while, as if lost in thought; he took a sip from the glass of Paradiso and shook his head. — No, no — he said — it's not the same thing.

— You should get used to the Manzanillo — the girl observed, groping for her eyebrow pencil in her tortoise-shell case. — It doesn't kill, simply washes away the memory of everything.

Afterwards you're like someone who has gone over to the other side and is no longer afraid of anything. But you want to remain in the ditch—fishing up the eels of your past.

The waiter came back with a sour look on his face.

— A Châteaubriand? — he asked. — A *velouté* of scampi 'in coppa'? A dozen or two snails *alla borgognona*? A slice of salmon from the Rhine? Or would you like to start with some woodcock?

— I wanted — the man replied gloomily — a small *beccafico* leg roasted on a wood fire and a sliver of eel pickled in soap. Pity, it's not possible. Can I have the bill, please? He took a long blue note from his wallet, left it on the plate and said to the girl:

— Shall we go? I promise next time I'll start with the Manzanillo too.

— But don't stop there — she said — one isn't enough. The best comes last.

Part II

Mr. Fuchs' Enemies

I had long been impressed by Mr. Fuchs' enemies. I didn't know them, but he often talked about them. Those in high positions as well as those obscure and modest, both men and women, how could they all hate such a monument of respectability, such a monster of learning, so disinterested a champion of snobbery? He was tall, slim, and shabbily dressed, with a long yellow moustache drooping over his greedy mouth. An accomplished linguist and well known in social and intellectual circles in Italy and elsewhere, Mr. Fuchs' age and origin were obscure. Penniless, like all true poets (for he considered himself as such even though he didn't write poetry) his main occupation was that of professional guest. He was always in search of rich and possibly aristocratic families, who could put at his disposal a room and two daily meals in a castle on the Loire, a tower in the Vosges, a villa in San Sebastian, or at worst an apartment in Florence, Venice or Milan. He looked for them and found them; or rather he used to find them. For after the last World War the rich handed over their castles to the State and the custom of offering patronage became increasingly rare. So that even the much sought-after Fuchs had at times to put up in fourth-class hotels and cook his own meals—consisting mostly of chops, beetroot, cheese and fruit—on a small spirit-stove. What would be quite a simple meal for you and me became for him something like the music of Mozart. Not a day passed without Mr. Fuchs revealing to his friends the ingredients of one of his concoctions. For, as well as enemies, Fuchs had also many friends who, though unable to invite him to a villa, invited him to restaurants and offered him a meal more sumptuous than his own. He was a master in the art of making the person who invited him believe that he had done himself an immense honour. Everyone fell into this trap and I was no exception. I had been his friend for some months and invited him more than once, either to my house or to a restaurant, as I was very much impressed by his witty and lively conversation. Then one day, in almost tragic circumstances, our friendship came to an end and I discovered the mystery I had long been so curious about.

It had been a very cold winter in Florence. Coal wasn't easily available or (I don't remember) the people who shared the house with me couldn't afford it. I used to heat my room with an electric fire, whose four elements functioned only in pairs.

I was having lunch with Fuchs when he showed signs of discomfort because of the heat. I got up and turned off two elements, which he considered superfluous. A little later he raised his moustache from the leg of mutton (a miracle from the black market) into which he was about to sink his teeth, to say that he was freezing. I immediately got up, apologised, and turned the fire full on. Scarcely a minute had passed before Fuchs observed that three, rather than two or four, elements would have created the ideal atmosphere for conversation.

— I'm sorry — I answered — I can't do anything about it, my fire only works on two or four elements. And it's the only one I've got.

We talked for some time and I kept getting up to turn the two switches on or off, but Mr. Fuchs had obviously become sulky, having lost all faith in my regulating ability. Finally he got up himself, bent over the stove and fiddled with it for some time, turning the switch in all directions. It went out with a sizzling hiss.

— It looks as if I've broken it — he said, raising his moustache from his handiwork.

— I hope not — I said — but in any case it doesn't matter. Let's go somewhere warmer and talk there.

He seemed terribly cross. — There are only two possibilities — he said. — Either I've broken it or I haven't, and you should either accept it or get it working again. Can't you do it? (I made one or two attempts, but to no avail.) — You see: it's broken and it's I who broke it.

— Don't worry — I said; — maybe it's only a valve. It's happened to me, too.

— What do you mean by that? — Mr. Fuchs asked — to you too? That amounts to saying that it's my fault this time.

— I'm not saying anything, Mr. Fuchs. The fire doesn't work; let's admit it's my fault, which it is really, since I don't have a better one. But the damage is negligible and it'll be repaired tomorrow.

— You're merely complicating matters by pretending to be guilty, when in fact what you are really suggesting is that it's I who am guilty. You realise that the word guilty is a serious one?

— I admit it's a serious word and I apologise, but I was actually using it with regard to myself, not you.

— Until the whole thing is cleared up, the word also concerns me. I arrived here a guest, and now I'm leaving a convicted man. I'm sure you'll agree that irreparable harm has been done to good manners. When I broke a looking-glass belonging to Princess Thurn und Taxis, the servant was dismissed and the looking-glass replaced at once. And at that time I really *was* guilty. But now the question is *sub judice*. Good-bye, I don't expect we shall meet again.

With a little nod he headed towards the door. I tried to restrain him but in vain. Unwillingly and without my intending it, I too was enrolled in the ever-growing ranks of his enemies. But I consoled myself with the thought that perhaps I was of more use to him that way.

71

Mr. Stapps

The story has an antecedent. Late one winter afternoon in 19— Mr. Lazarus Young, M.A., Ph.D., a very small shy man, who always wore a flat hat with a magpie's feather in it, saw a little sparrow lying on a heap of snow on a street in the Bronx, New York. It was completely stiff and barely alive. In trying to save the sickly bird he missed the transatlantic boat that was bound for Europe. Through the care of eminent specialists the bird's life was saved and it was given the luxury of a heated cage specially made for it. All this, together with missing the *Jacques Cartier*, cost Mr. Young two or three thousand dollars. And now Snow Flake (Snow for short) had with its wrinkled skin, acquired a venerable appearance; it used to surprise visitors to the villa at No. 48 Erta Canina, Florence, where Mr. Young used to spend a month every five years, leaving behind his gardener and his cook.

The year I happened to meet Mr. Young, he had to leave the city in haste after an unusually brief stay, to return to his hometown Saint Louis (Missouri) and thus escape an atmosphere which he found intolerable. However, he left behind a rather strange guest to look after Snow: Mr. Josef Stapps, a big, fat fellow, somewhere between forty and sixty, with blue eyes, freshly shaven chubby cheeks crossed by a network of bluish veins, always looking very dandified in his big bell-shaped raglan, with hair fashionably cut, and fingers covered in cameo rings. He carried an inlaid walking stick, wore kangaroo gloves, silk muffler and handkerchiefs, and always had a cigarette-case, Dunhill pipe and things like that.

Mr. Stapps was installed in the oblong blue room which had a connecting bathroom, and four large porthole-like windows overlooking olive trees and the street-side of the garden. He had decided to spend the whole of that grisly post-war period there. Incidentally it is worth mentioning our friendship, which started purely by accident. If the love affairs of others, and especially those of our friends, seem quite incomprehensible and senseless, the same could be said about friendships. Even here we tend to be prejudiced and moralistic. *A man is known by the company* . . . etc. And yet the implication is profoundly unjust. For each one of us has had at least one friend whom one would like to be able to justify to oneself and yet cannot.

For me such a friend was Mr. Stapps. According to him I was the only man in the world he had condescended to associate with, although he was no misanthrope and never failed to allude to the high-class company he frequented, and to old ties and intimate connections with people of another international and elusive sphere, which was fast disappearing. However, the fact is that for six months I was the only person he saw in Florence; and he too was my only companion in that long and enervating period of waiting for an end of the world that did not come, or that came six or seven years later. How was it possible that one solitary man, and a mediocre one at that, could have taken the place of an entire universe? And yet my good friend Stapps, the only guardian left in a city which used to be one of the centres of European civilisation, was not unequal to the task I had mentally assigned to him.

To tell the truth, Mr. Stapps was a man whose origins and way of living were rather obscure. He claimed to be a Bohemian, to have been married three times, to have belonged to the world of Czech diplomacy, and to have quarrelled with his friends Masaryk and Benes. However, he did not know the language of his own country nor did he speak any other language which I knew. He talked to me in a mixture of bad English and bad French or in a still more complicated Esperanto. — I have *delivrato* the pigeon — he told me the day he had freed his hawk. In the Young establishment he had no contact with the servants. A perfect cook, he cooked for himself in the daytime, improvising succulent dishes. And in the evening he would eat with me in cave-like trattorias, draining huge carafes of Chianti, and eating the most exotic salads. Late at night, when he had walked home through the haunted park, he would sit down at his desk and work.

What sort of work? That he could be a writer was out of the question because of the linguistic drawback already mentioned. He seemed to know a miscellany of poets from all over the world from T'ang to Rilke, in the original text—a sort of handy anthology in the manner of one who like Robinson felt himself to be the sole survivor of a threatened culture. In any case Stapps, half adventurer, half dandy, was a dedicated priest of such a culture, and perhaps this was the bond that united us. In a city of lies, swastikas and German books, Mr. Stapps, with his gold teeth and fatuously false forty-year-old smile, kept 'delivering' hawks, pasting up Sumerian poems, feeding Snow Flake on hypophosphates and preparing his famous stews, as unconcerned as ever. Wrapped up in a cloud of allusions, reserve, worldliness and bad literature, he, Josef Stapps, was there, in his place, and so long as he was there, I felt tolerably hopeful.

One late afternoon in autumn Antonio Delfini and I went up to the villa to taste a new species of *goulash* which he had offered to President Stambolijski, at Neuilly, in 19—. Climbing dreamily through the orchards and gardens, eating the meal that he had cooked and which we ourselves served, put new life into us, so that a beakful of yellow paprika stew was even allowed to the poor half-blind Snow, eternally chirping in his boiler room. Afterwards there was lively conversation, gramophone music, liqueurs, and finally camomile tea. At midnight the festivities were interrupted to listen for Gilly the ghost passing over the gravel with his wheelbarrow. I too heard him and shivered. Later on Antonio and I staggered home, our throats burning, but convinced that, against all odds, Mr. Stapps twice a day—at midday and at dinner—rendered homage to a drowning deity.

That was the last time I saw Mr. Stapps. And the period during which I had needed him was drawing to a close, and the anthems of victory were within earshot. A few evenings later I noticed that the room with the portholes was shut. The agent of the Young family told me that Mr. Stapps had left suddenly and that he had asked to be remembered to me. Since then I have heard nothing.

As for poor Snow, the wretched bird was unable to survive the change in its regimen prescribed for him by an ornithologist from Johns Hopkins University. The following day it was found dead, rolled into a ball on the bar of its heated cage. The agent said it was exactly eleven years and three months old. Before he went away, Mr. Stapps buried it with his own hands under the foot of a tree that Gilly, with his wheelbarrow, was wont, every evening, to pass.

Dominico

In those days a letter from Dominico in Brazil used to be the big event in my life. The letter would be in that special language of his, half-American, half-Sicilian, which made conversation with him so difficult. And so you can imagine what it must have been like now that he had acquired some knowledge of Brazilian!

— *Write me* — he said — *una vostra lettera sera* [*sic*] *muito desejada por min.* And only yesterday I found a photo of Dominico taken during his stay in Florence some ten years ago, together with a group of bigshots. In a city where almost every day some new exhibition was opened or some other vaguely cultural ceremony took place, followed by refreshments, Dominico, always keen on the odd invitation (for gastronomical reasons), was one of the most popular and most photographed people there. Nobody knew his name, but there was no party or 'gathering' (a word very much in use in those days) where Dominico was not found sitting right in the front row, smiling in the harsh magnesium light with a delicious puff pastry in his hand.

And here he was in this *fotomontage*, sitting beside the prefect and the secretary of the Fascist federation, in his typical yellow jersey, a pair of worn-out trousers and a pair of gaping sandals, with his long moustache drooping round his large fleshy mouth. His Mongolian eyes were lit up with pleasure as he saw all around him, enumerated in huge letters, the virtues of Florence as a university city, its eighteen-hole golf courses, its picturesque sightseeings, its firework displays, grape festivals at Impruneta and other marvels.

A beautiful world, Dominico thought, so long as it lasted; and so very pleasant to feel oneself half Italian, without cares and without responsibilities, protected by an American passport and a light cultural luggage in which Dante and Lorenzo de'Medici, Garibaldi and Mazzini figured along with the names of Lincoln and Jefferson, Whitman and Ulysses Grant, forming a very appetising sight indeed, a retrospective *coup d'oeil* on a universe lit up with the glare of the new imagist poetry of which Dominico Braga, the American grocer's son who had emigrated from Linguaglossa to Bridgeport, claimed to be, after Ezra Pound, the most conspicuous representative. He knew very little Italian, and his knowledge of English was not much better. His actual mother tongue was the Linguaglossa dialect, but even this he had by now almost forgotten. And yet at the age of twenty or so he felt 'the call of Italy', the call of his motherland, and set out as an apprentice scullery-boy on a cargo boat which took him to Holland. During the voyage, by a stroke of luck, the ship's baker, an inveterate pessimist and an avid reader of Schopenhauer and Hartmann, committed suicide by throwing himself overboard, and so Dominico took over his job. Consequently, when he arrived in Amsterdam, he had saved enough money to buy a motor-cycle, *Pegaso*, on which he travelled across Europe. But in San Bernardo his motor-cycle collided with a cow and by way of compensation Dominico had to hand over the remains of his ramshackle vehicle to the owner of the wounded animal and continue his journey on foot.

In Florence the yellow jersey became immediately popular and within a few days Dominico had become the most voracious consumer of bigné ever seen at public functions. He actually lived on it and only on rare occasions did he touch the mine-strone served by the friars of the local monasteries. There was something unreal about the life in a city full of students and foreigners, which pleased Dominico. His vaguely democratic principles did not prevent him from enjoying the sort of carnival régime that the Italians in those days had subjected themselves to, and which he considered to be perfectly in tune with the Palio, with football (which was starting to be fashion-able in those days), and with other local manifestations. 'Paese che vai'—and Dominico was not the sort of man to go in very much for the deeper and subtler aspects of things, and all the more so because his Master, Ezra, had assured him that the only thing lacking in Italy was peanut plantations; otherwise Italy would be a model country for 'a permanent and efficient totalitarian democracy'.

After all what had we to complain about? Dominico Braga paid no heed to the grumbling of his new friends. He liked everything about our country, especially the mass spectacles and open-air shows in the Boboli gardens. He made it a point never to miss them, without, however, thinking it necessary to pay for his ticket; he would emerge from the bushes and get mixed up with the sprites evoked by the producer Reinhardt, so that one would invariably find him in his yellow jersey, sitting smiling in the first row. One day there was trouble, when two new friends, unfortunately introduced by me, called on him in his dismal attic in Via Panicale. The three had to sleep together in a small bed, Braga, the proletarian writer Morluschi, and the Bulgarian painter Angelof. But during the night, angry voices ('Gangster! Swine! Spy!') reached the printers living on the floor below, which made them think that a violent ideological quarrel had broken out among the three rascals. Between one spell of sleep and another the two guests had discovered that Dominico belonged to the abhorrent reactionary forces and so they tried to throw him out. But they made it up again. Perhaps their sense of the ridiculous contributed to the reconciliation more than any political conviction. . . . A few days later, Dominico left Florence.

I later learnt that he continued leading a 'free' life in America, managing to publish his prose and verse every four years or so in the ephemeral magazines which flourish in every State during the pre-election days.

What could my *muito desejada* letter tell him today? Linguistic difficulties are nothing compared with those arising from a different spiritual background. Could I make him understand what was happening in Italy today? With his pure and innocent soul, Dominico Braga was one of those men who, without a nationality, without confines, defying all conventions and the laws of the Utopian classics and deprived of a nationality, make humanity something difficult to understand, let alone desire. People like him can escape from the constituted order, can evade the network of history, simply because the majority conforms. Moreover, how far can the liberty of a single man, a liberty that not every man can possess, be of interest to us? My feeling is that by thinking only in terms of his own salvation, Dominico had damned himself. A man without any religious sense of collective life can't but miss what is best in individual life, in the life of a man. A man is nothing in isolation. But it would be painful to explain such a thing to Dominico, especially in a language which I should have to invent for him and at a time when any form of downright egoism, any form of anarchy, seems preferable to the social and materialistic obsessions of the big powers who concern themselves from afar with us and with our unhappy peninsula. . . .

Alastor's Visit

In the cold, deserted suburban street, the appearance of the Lincoln belonging to Patrick O'C had attracted some attention. The person who got out of it—a tall, fat man with thin reddish-grey hair, robust, but no longer young—consulted his address book and found out from a grocer the address of the house he was looking for: number 117, on the right-hand staircase in Via delle Stringhe, a rather shabby house in an inner courtyard where one could hear boys yelling and famished dogs yelping. Could Ponzio Macchi, the most assiduous and perhaps the ablest of his foreign translators, possibly live there? There was no doubt this was the house whose address and number he had been given. Patrick O'C felt mildly surprised. The registry office of the good souls has its mysteries and life is sometimes hard for those who do not follow in the tracks of the great human herds. Patrick O'C—known throughout the civilised world under his pseudonym Alastor—tried to remind himself of this maxim as he drank a glass of *grappa*. After giving the grocer a handsome tip, and having asked him, more by gesture than with words, to keep an eye on his car, he went to the staircase, at the top of which there was a brass name-plate with Ponzio Macchi's name. The woman who came to open the door after he had knocked a few times (the bell must have been out of order) had a surly look and carried a snivelling child in her arms. She must have been the translator's wife—a pale figure, carelessly dressed and of uncertain age. Was the gentleman, or rather the professor in? Yes, no, yes—it was difficult to know since Patrick could not speak a word of Italian and the supposed Mrs. Macchi was not familiar with any of the languages he knew. The Irish-American handed her a visiting card with his name and a long string of qualifications (M.A., Ph.D. and others) printed on it in capital letters, followed by the name Alastor pencilled in brackets.

Alastor was ushered into a cold room where at least four of

his own volumes could be seen among the books on a small shelf, and then had to wait for some time. As he entered, the tapping sound of the typewriter in the next room stopped. Perhaps the 'professor' was working? Alastor shivered with cold as he stood there.

Some minutes passed. He heard voices discussing something animatedly. Then he heard the sound of a window being closed, after which there was complete silence. A moment later the lady he had supposed to be Signora Macchi appeared, and Alastor was taken into the room of his worthy translator. The room was dark, as the shutters were closed. In the electric light he could see a man lying in bed, with a worn woollen scarf wrapped round his head. From a heap of ragged blankets a pale face emerged. On the marble top of the bedside table stood a pile of manuscripts, perhaps a new translation of one of Alastor's own books.

The wife of the sick man stayed on to listen to the conversation. After a bow, Alastor asked if the person in front of him was Professor Macchi (*yes*, was the answer), and if he was really so unfortunate as to find him ill (*yes*). He started by apologising for the awkward time of his visit (*yes*), at the same time expressing his gratitude for the translation and publicity to which Ponzio Macchi (yes, yes) had dedicated a considerable part of his time and energy which could have been better spent otherwise (yes, oh yes). Did he enjoy company at all? Alastor went on. Or did he want to be left alone? Did he need medicines, help, advice? Was he in the hands of a good doctor? Would he like him to pay another visit? Or would he rather not? To all these questions the answer was, *yes*. Alastor thought it was time for him to go and so with another bow he left his translator's room.

He then took leave of the woman who did not seem particularly pleased to be called Mrs. Macchi. She accompanied him as far as the staircase. A little later the American ordered himself another glass of *grappa* at the grocer's, and then quietly started his big Lincoln.

As he left, he was observed from 117, right-hand staircase, Via delle Stringhe, through the slats of the still half-closed shutters, by Ponzio Macchi who had in the meantime got up and dressed, by his wife and by the three children who were quite excited about his visit.

— Seems to have come out of the blue — Ponzio said, as he wiped his forehead. — And without knowing a word of Italian, silly fool! What on earth is he going to do next? Did he say he was coming back?

— If he did, you'd lie down again in bed, wouldn't you? — his wife inquired maliciously.

— Well, if he does, tell him I'm away, and that I won't be back for at least two months. That's not much to ask, is it? You can say it in a couple of words. I'll teach you.

— If you'd known any words yourself, you wouldn't have cut such a sorry figure, you blockhead.

— I did keep talking, didn't I, you cow? Actually I not only managed, but managed very well.

— Idiot, it would do you good if you started doing some work. I'll deal with him if he comes back. You'd be better off pretending to be a deaf-mute.

In the meantime Patrick O'C was driving to his hotel. He was to leave the day after. He gave no more thought to his translator. But had he stumbled on the unlikely truth that in that malingering fraud there was a character worthy of one of his own short stories, then nothing would have deterred him from ferreting it out.

Honey

Sir Donald L. loved travelling, especially in Italy. His long life had been spent pretty comfortably—or at any rate the first half of it, which was lived in the heyday of the Edwardian era. It was the life of a man on the up and up in a country that was on the up and up—a life that was never marred by any doubt about oneself or one's place in society. He was the son of a Newcastle brewer, possibly half-Jewish by birth, but not quite rich enough to be able to avail himself from the outset of the advantages of his birth. Having delicate health from early childhood and with no precocious talent, he was received at Eton with a certain diffidence and while there was repeatedly beaten by his seniors. He took a tolerable degree from Oxford after four years of struggle with tutors and other undergraduates with whom he was not particularly popular, and then entered the Civil Service from which he retired at the end of the first World War. He acquired a title which made him desire to live among his own kind—i.e. among the gentry. From that period date his long travels as a self-styled man from the North who feels the call of the South: Greece, Spain, Morocco, the Balearic Islands, the Azores, and above all Italy, which he knew from top to toe: southern Italy, especially, where he wrote his books (which nobody has ever heard of) and where his first friends are or rather were to be found. But times have changed—social and political revolutions, which he, of course, abhorred, have brought about an interminable crisis; the folly of an Italian dictator who at first seemed so mild and 'charming', but later turned out to be so cruel, another World War that seemed to go on for ever and ever, and the coming to power of an English government which imposed irksome financial restrictions—all these things obliged Sir Donald to pass year after year (the last and most precious part of his life) in a gloomy three-room flat, full of books and memories, but lacking in sunshine and human warmth.

The flat was in St. John's Wood, where at least there is no lack of greenery. Each house has its own tiny garden, surrounded by trees. It is not far from the heart of the city and this city is in turn the heart of the best-organised and most civilised society left in the world. And yet Sir Donald felt a prisoner there, and the need for someone with whom he could admire and at the same time ridicule the complex hierarchy of which he regarded himself as one of the ornaments. Who could he turn to? Certainly not to the middle-class young men who visited him: painters, pseudo-writers, semi-parasites, ready to offer him their advice, to drive his Austin (on rationed petrol), to eat up his food, and in general to exploit his miserable position as a bachelor who couldn't live alone. No, despite their uses, these provided few consolations. An Italian passing through the city, an Italian young enough to enable Sir Donald to say, 'I, when you were still a baby . . .' and sufficiently educated to be able to sustain the offensive of an almost Platonic dialogue: that was what he was looking for.

For forty-eight hours I filled that role. The first day he took me round the city, apologising for not being a perfect guide. (In Italy, of course, it would have been different; there he would, no doubt, have been all one could wish for; what did I, a young whipper-snapper, know about the real Italy?) He made a point of showing me everything he regarded as being particularly awful or grand: docks, slums, the changing of the guard at Buckingham Palace, old inns and chemists' shops with seventeenth-century ceilings or lattice work, antique shops, his club, endless parks and gardens, in which the recently imported grey squirrels had devoured the red ones which used to be there, and where even the number of grey squirrels was rapidly going down. I told him that red squirrels were delicious. I had eaten one myself in Italy. At this point we changed the subject and began to discuss the arts of the kitchen.

Sir Donald was so annoyed that I should be taken in by those advertisements with their plates full of carrots, and yellow sauce bottles labelled 'perfect for soup' that he decided to invite me to dinner and thus prove that even someone of his background and upbringing, used to better things, could fend for himself in reduced circumstances. He would demonstrate there and then. No, he decided, after a moment's thought, not there and then, that was asking too much. After all the thing needed some preparation and forethought. There was no point in going to a restaurant, still less to an Italian *trattoria*, though in his company there was no question of being cheated. He suggested, instead, that I should come to his house. Not that evening, of course! It was out of the question. He had to inform his cook Honey who lived in Manchester, but who came down every so often to prepare food for him. Was it too far? Oh no, a mere four hours train journey. A telegram would do the trick; his sweet Honey would be there next morning, and would have plenty of time to have the banquet ready that evening. I was told to come a bit earlier—about seven o'clock. I asked if I could bring an Italian friend with me. Yes, even two if I liked. I was dropped at my hotel where I had to content myself with a meagre supper. But the next day. . . .

The next day at half-past six I was standing at the corner of Oxford Street and Park Lane, vainly trying to get some taxi-driver to take pity on me. But it was useless. At that time of the day it is practically impossible to find a taxi in London. In despair, I gave a hotel porter with a more piercing whistle than mine a couple of bob and begged him to help me. At seven o'clock my friend Alberto Moravia and I were climbing the narrow staircase of Sir Donald's flat and shortly afterwards we met Honey. The angel that had arrived from a coal-black city was herself black as coal. She was one of those women who, when questioned about their age, answer 'ty-five', leaving a blank space between thirty-five and up-wards—with no limit; round, fat, greasy, curly and amiable. Sir Donald and his pals were standing together, laughing and chatting. Everybody was introduced and praised—she, the guests and the food that was now ready. Honey was not in the kitchen, as one might have expected. Perhaps everything had been prepared and was keeping hot on the stove. She herself appeared to be of mixed origins—forthright, jolly, and quick to respond to every allusion and innuendo. It wasn't easy though, to follow her conversation because of her Cockney accent. However, nothing stopped my friend Alberto and me from splitting our sides, partly out of politeness to the host, and partly because several cocktails had put us in a good mood. Dinner was casually referred to: *hors-d'oeuvre* with gull's eggs (which were not rationed), roast chicken, a delicious fruit tart. Unfortunately someone had turned on the television and there was a play on that seemed to interest Honey and all those present. It was a thriller of some sort.

I took the opportunity of going downstairs, where Alberto joined me. We were a bit worried.

— Gull's eggs! — I said — There's nothing to be done. They're as black as Honey and very salty.

— Let's hope the chicken isn't roast seagull — Alberto joked. From the other room one could hear shouts and laughter.

— Murder, murder — Honey was shouting frantically. We went down to the courtyard and for about half an hour nobody seemed to notice our absence or call to us. The drama was about to reach its climax. Honey was alternately emitting shrieks and sobs, and then at a certain point the shouts grew milder, followed by a sudden silence, and a little later by the sound of people trying to bring someone round. The thriller must have come to an end or been interrupted, we thought. We hurried upstairs to join them.

The lights were turned on. Honey was lying half-undressed on the sofa. Everyone was standing around her, fanning her or smacking her on the cheek. She had enjoyed the play enormously, but the coming back to life of the corpse in the trunk had been too much for her and she had fainted. We would have to hurry through dinner and then take her to her son who lived close by—i.e. about half an hour's run by car. Unfortunately, the dinner was roasting in the electric oven. Never mind, it could be reheated. Three young dandies brought up hard-boiled eggs from the kitchen—eggs with dark mottled shells and their insides completely green from being overcooked. Sir Donald suggested that they were not worth eating. It would be better to make do with the chicken which at least was genuine, though burnt to a cinder in its bed of pickles and radishes. The tart, on the other hand, wasn't at all bad and one could drink as much Australian wine as one wanted. It was getting late and we had to leave. Honey was herself again and ready to set out. Everyone kissed her behind the ear and assured her that she was a marvellous cook. One of the young men went out to call a taxi. We divided into two groups, each going in the opposite direction. Sir Donald, Honey and two of the young men were going in the Austin; the other two guests, Alberto and I, would take the taxi as far as the next tube station. This we did, parting with smiles and handshakes. Going down on the escalator I happened to look at my watch: it was twenty past eleven—too late to find any restaurant open. And we hadn't even remembered to thank our host.

Clizia at Foggia

The railway lines glittered under the torrid sky of Foggia. Above them the mushed-grape-coloured coaches, the dry fountain, the tree trunks tied to each other (an absurd anticipation of winter) seemed on the point of melting like rubber. A brief but vivid glimpse of the buffer of the train as it moved gently away almost led one to think that after a hundred yards or so one could catch up with the last coach. But during those brief seconds that Clizia spent calculating her remaining strength, which had suffered from two long days in the sultry heat of Foggia, the hundred yards became a hundred and fifty, then two hundred. It was three o'clock in the afternoon. Perched cautiously on the edge of a seat in the waiting-room, Clizia opened the railway time-table and studied it—only to find that there were no trains before seven. And then there was only a slow one taking twenty long hours to carry her north. Instinctively she raised her eyes to heaven, desperate, but at the same time resigned, like those who in the face of extreme danger look skyward. But the ceiling of the waiting-room didn't open up to admit any consoling spirit. Instead there appeared, in all its shabby and dismal pomp, a canopy of yellow fly-catcher, the black dots buzzing in concerted anguish. In the middle of the nearest confection one could see a dark spider becalmed in stickiness. How had it got there? After considering various alternatives, Clizia came to the conclusion that a gust of wind had brought about this catastrophe. While hanging by its thread, the spider must have dropped down through the gaps in its airy architecture, and then got caught up in the squall, which had hurled it on to the fatal quicksands.

Having reached this conclusion Clizia went out into the square. Although her fibre suitcase was small and light, it still caused her hand to burn as if she'd been stung. In summer the bars are not the most comfortable places to go to because of the blowflies which divide their attentions equally between the customers and what they're consuming. Clizia, however, had already vacated her room in the hotel. For a moment she wasn't sure what to do. But then she had a brilliant idea while she was looking at a green poster on the wall. In the Municipal hall (and she immediately saw in her mind a cool place with soft arm-chairs) two eminent professors, Dobrowsky and Peterson, from the university of Bâton Rouge and the Avatar Institute of Charleston (South Carolina) were to take part in an important debate on metempsychosis. And if a member of the public were to volunteer, there would also be invaluable practical experiments. The cost of admission was only a few lira.

A little later Clizia walked through a gate decorated with scrubby lemons and pine leaves. Arrows pointed the way. She found the shade in the corridors quite refreshing. In the hall about fifteen people were seated at a discreet distance from the table where the two speakers were already installed. The two men were very different: one bald, lean, bespectacled, and dressed in a dark suit; the other fat and ruddy, dressed in shorts and a shirt of raw silk.

An attendant (or perhaps a disciple) was going round selling pamphlets; Clizia bought one. On the first page there was a picture of Pythagoras in the temple of Apollo at Branchide. His arm came out of his toga and pointed to a shield on the wall. A white cloud rose from his square masculine face which was like the faces of the young people around him, bearing this inscription in block letters: 'This is the shield I used when I was Euforbo and Menelaus wounded me!' Inside the booklet the episode was explained in detail and there were also brief notes on the life and work of the great philosopher. Clizia read two or three pages, but her novice's zeal gradually waned as the coolness of the hall gave way to stuffiness and flies.

She moved and sat in a dark corner a few rows back in order to avoid the searching glance of Professor Peterson. In this way she gradually lost contact with the external world, and plunged into a light but not disagreeable coma.

At first she felt as if there were no longer any force of gravity in the world. She felt weightless as if resting on eight very long and soft hairy paws which deadened the noise of her steps. That is, if one could talk of steps, for as she proceeded, there were no steps, but fractions of steps propelled first by one, then by another paw, in a regular movement beyond her control. She saw the world in a horizontal rather than a vertical perspective, as used to happen, she remembered, when she tried to walk on stilts. Not only did the position of her body, which was bent forward, more or less like a soldier in an 'open order' exercise, contribute to her new vision, but also the strange disposition of her eyes, of which she had eight, forming a semi-circle round her head. As a result, a large part of the plain around her seemed to enlarge simultaneously her illusion of space and liberty. Two of her eyes suffered in the harsh glare of the daylight. But even this helped her to feel a greater measure of freedom, because, with the lengthening of the evening shadows, these eyes came into their own and lit up the shadows with startling clarity.

She had before her a beautiful, detailed and well-worn canvas. So beautiful was it that she could penetrate the four walls of the tiny marbled courtyard in the midst of which a little fountain played night and day, scattering its water on to a layer of soft moss. A young man dressed in white came now and then for a stroll in the courtyard (but where had she seen him before?). He held a book in his hand and glanced at it from time to time as he walked up and down, oblivious of everything around him. Sometimes he stopped and looked at the canvas. Once he even came into the light to look at it. The young man seemed to be impressed by the beautiful effect of the dew upon the delicate tissues of the moonlit web. And as he looked, the canvas appeared to be almost a continuation of his thoughts, an integral part of the book he was reading as he walked along the arcades from dawn till dusk.

At times friends came to visit this young man with the beautiful face. They sat with him by the fountain, or on the steps round the portico, and occasionally just where Clizia sat. They talked as they turned over the pages of books and parchments. Their gestures caused tiny ripples of air which sent waves through the canvas so that for a second they awakened the entangled flies which were by now quite stunned and passive. Often the group would munch something, and after they'd left, the spider would come down to collect its booty of crumbs, fruit-peel and grapes. One hot afternoon the spider caught sight of a row of plates full of a sweet, yellow, strongly-scented pulp lying on the steps, and greedily lowered itself further and further, extending its silken ladder, until suddenly it realised the danger and pulled up short. But it was too late. The soft golden nectar had already claimed it, and though it swung, tossed, spat out all its entrails in an attempt to strengthen the thread and climb back, its fate was sealed. First its head was firmly caught and then a leg. A sweetish, sickly smell formed around it, and its body became hard. At its last gasp, it was about to throw its head back to hasten its end when a hand gently took her by the arm and woke her up.

She saw the man in shorts and the man in the dark suit bending over her.

— Signora — said the former — you're really a most exceptional subject. Would you like to come up on the platform and tell us what you dreamt. Your name, profession and anything else about yourself? Do you live in this town? Do you work, study or travel?

— No, I sing — Clizia replied, just by way of saying something (in fact she often did sing to herself).

— Ladies and gentlemen — thundered Professor Dobrowsky, in the most excruciating Italian, and turning to the audience — perhaps we have a reincarnation of the Malibran or of the divine Sappho. But no, it's impossible, it would have been too big a leap in time. Would you like to tell us, Signora, *who* you dreamt you were? Your dream will be a clue to your previous existence. Let yourself go, please talk freely.

Clizia looked about her and saw that the number of those present had increased from fifteen to thirty.

— Well — she said, a feeling of extreme embarrassment mingling with a sense of outraged modesty — well, I think I dreamt I had become a spider, yes, a spider in the courtyard of Pythagoras, for I seemed to have recognised his face.

The audience burst into laughter and Professor Dobrowsky turned red in the face.

— Signora — he said — you're making fun of science, you don't deserve the sympathetic reaction my hypnosis created in you. You realise one would have to be perfect to pass from a spider to a human being? Be serious, tell us *what* you dreamt you were.

— A spider in Pythagoras's courtyard — Clizia repeated; scornful laughter echoing all round her. At this, Professor Peterson took her by the arm and accompanied her to the door, cautioning her not to take part in experiments that were too far above her.

Clutching her suitcase angrily, she ran out into the street. There, humming a tune to herself to re-establish her identity, she looked at her wrist-watch. A quarter of an hour to wait before the train was due. Her afternoon in Foggia was almost over.

The Stormy One

The news that Giampaolo had married Mrs. Dirce F., who had twice been a widow and was much older than he, hadn't given rise to any unfavourable comments in the town. Giampaolo's had been a trying life, and to know that he had now finally settled down (even though at the expense of certain inevitable sacrifices) was a source of relief to his many friends. The wedding was followed by sumptuous feasting and celebrations, after which the life of the couple entered a quieter phase. They were still talked about but in a somewhat ambiguous way. It was said that Giampaolo 'worked'—though it was never mentioned quite what sort of work it was—and that Dirce had created an earthly paradise for him. It was obvious though that the pair were living slightly cut off from the rest of the town. Those who mentioned them at all used to refer to not very recent meetings and invitations, and even though they praised the fine quality of the dishes prepared by the signora and her generous hospitality, they showed no desire to repeat the experience, rather, if anything, to avoid it. What these cautious people said never amounted to a criticism or reservation as such; and yet an odd kind of evasive constraint could be observed on the faces of those who continued to describe them in such terms as 'the signora Dirce . . . Giampaolo . . . a splendid couple . . .'.

Federigo had not realised the nature of these excuses until one morning, wandering absent-mindedly through Via del Forno, he came to No. 15 and remembered that his old friend Giampaolo had moved there. Federigo was both shy and poor, and he felt he had no business entering Giampaolo's new life and picking up the crumbs from the feast. Although a friendly sort, he was in no way a hanger-on or a parasite. Thus a mixture of reserve and pride prevented him from approaching his more fortunate friend; until at last the ice was broken by sheer chance and Federigo found himself, without even realising it, on the point of ringing the bell of Giampaolo's house, in the expectation of half an hour of agreeable chat.

Greeted with snarls from a watch dog and ushered into a vast room—which he soon learned to call the 'living room'— full of paintings, statues, pewter vases and silver eagles— Federigo, the moment after an ill-shaven servant had communicated his full particulars to the proper quarters, was enthusiastically received by the Signora herself.

Federigo Bezzica? What an unexpected honour! For years, for two or three years in the early stages of his friendship with Giampaolo, when the good soul, the second good soul, was still alive (a finger was raised to indicate a bald man in a large oil portrait) she, signora Dirce, had learnt everything about him, and was full of admiration for his life and character. Federigo Bezzica! If only she'd known him before. . . . Who knows. . . . The dearest, the most dignified, the most reserved of Giampaolo's friends. Surely it was he who was to blame for being the last to show up. Shyness? Love of a quiet life? She, of course, understood (oh, how much!) his taste for 'blessed solitude', it was on the basis of such an affinity that she hoped to establish a solid friendship with him. Giampaolo? Yes, Giampaolo was working, but would come up in a moment. In the meanwhile they could talk a little and get to know each other better. Can I offer you a port, a dry Martini, a Negroni? Fabrizio, where's that lazy Fabrizio got to? Hurry, bring a glass of port for this gentleman.

Federigo hadn't seen her properly yet. The drawing-room was in semi-darkness and the woman was sitting so close that he couldn't even turn his head. . . . But a huge mirror—a *trumeau* she called it—threw back an image of a strange bird of prey, beak vibrating, with hair somewhere between blue and mahogany and burning eyes. She lit her eyes up in the same way as one flicks a lighter to light someone's cigarette. Then turned them off.

After some time Giampaolo entered in shirt-sleeves, went up to them and kissed his wife's hands. He dared not say much.

In their turn, pale, thin and diffident, Antenore and Gontrano, the children of her first husband (the finger was again lifted to show the portrait of a moustached officer), and Rosemarie, the daughter of her second, came forward. It was already one o'clock. Signora Dirce decided that Federigo should stay and take pot-luck with them. They moved in to the dining-room. A delicate piece of embroidery was spread over a glass table over-hung by a bronze statue which seemed to be diving down on the guests. After the host had put on his jacket, Fabrizio started serving—a cup of consommé, a cheese soufflé, fried prawns, baby marrows, and a small basket of dried fruit. For coffee they went back to the 'living-room'. The filtering process took ages and the choice of liqueurs was equally painstaking. When Antenore, Gontrano and Rosemarie asked permission to go, Federigo was about to stand up and say good-bye too, but having at an unguarded moment expressed the desire to have a nap (a sensible after-lunch habit and one shared by Signora Dirce herself) he was almost literally forced to lie down on the sofa in the living-room and told to make himself at home. He remained in the dark for two hours, feeling rather apprehensive. There wasn't a sound to be heard; perhaps everybody was having a nap.

What could he do? The two hours seemed interminable. But the sound of the clock striking four bucked him up. He got up, opened a shutter, tidied the sofa he had lain on, and then tiptoed out in search of the front door. But he failed to escape the vigilant Fabrizio, with the result that a further shower of offers was heaped on him from the inner recesses of the living-room.

It was nearly tea-time. Why leave so soon? Urgent business? I don't believe it. Was he not feeling well? He should take a tonic. Perhaps some intro-muscular injections? The same as she used to give Giampaolo. Had his doctor prescribed it for him too? So much the better. No, there was no point in putting it off. No need to go to a chemist's. She would do everything herself since she was a trained nurse and a very good one at that. No formality between friends, for heaven's sake. It wouldn't take a minute.

She returned fully armed; Federigo was forced to stretch out on a pile of cushions and uncover an inch or two of his body for her to administer the injection. Completely worn out, he thought it his duty to stay a little longer. In the meantime Fabrizio had returned with the tea-trolley. Giampaolo now joined them.

He announced that the weather had suddenly taken a turn for the worse. It was raining. And Federigo hadn't even got an umbrella.

Signora Dirce immediately made up her mind. Federigo was to stay to dinner. It was no trouble at all; in fact it would be a great pleasure for everybody. And he was not going to say no. Unthinkable. If he did, it would be a declaration of war, wouldn't it! (Her eyes gleamed menacingly and Federigo made only a weak gesture of protest.)

But no, he was not going to refuse; he would stay. The rain was pelting down. Antenore and Gontrano had returned with the dog. Vermouth was served, and after another hour of pleasant chat, Fabrizio came back in white cotton gloves and announced that dinner was ready. Federigo was taken by the arm and led to his place, where a sumptuous soup, rabbit in aspic and peaches in syrup were awaiting him. Fabrizio was in attendance, grating Parmesan cheese over the soup. The conversation turned to love, and after the children had left, it became still more interesting. At ten o'clock thunder and lightning shook the whole house.

It was impossible to leave in such weather. Fabrizio would of course have taken him home in the car, but unfortunately he hadn't yet managed to get the differential repaired. But never mind. The guest-room was done up with loving care. She had furnished it herself. Would he like camomile or peppermint tea or a sleeping pill? They would meet the next morning at breakfast. But before that, at about eight, Fabrizio was instructed to take him a cup of black coffee in his room.

Did he need anything else? The bath-room was on the right, the light switch on the left. And thanks for a most delightful visit—the first, no doubt, of many. Thanks, thanks again; good-night, good-night.

It had stopped raining. Leaning out of the window of his room, Federigo realised that it would be dangerous to jump. Moreover, there was the gate to be negotiated too, the hazard of the fierce dog Tombolo, and other possible obstacles. And what if they took him for a burglar?

Uncertain what to do, he shut the window, taking in as he did so the pyjamas of the second (or perhaps the first) husband laid out on the bed. He picked them up at arm's length, only to drop them hurriedly at the sound of a knock at the door. It was Giampaolo, with a pair of old slippers.

— See you tomorrow then — he said — On the late side though, as I've work to do. And now when are you going to get married?

The Women of Karma

The visitor used to remember 'little Micky' (now called Donna Michelangiola) as being very slim, with long ash-blond hair falling over her shoulders and a light, firm step that betrayed a joyful, almost triumphant optimism. In those days her walk used to be—perhaps because of her high-heeled shoes—what one might call a *joie-de-vivre* walk, like that of Ibsen's Nora. But now? A short time ago, the visitor watched her as he stood behind a pillar. Like all her friends her nails were darkly enamelled, or enamelled with such a thick varnish that it seemed dark. Moreover she had a face that nothing in the world could make laugh and that bore an expression of in-human tedium and gloom. Like her friends she went about in a pair of ramshackle sandals like a friar's, that were worn down at the sides and too big for her. She had grown fatter, had short, straight dusty-grey hair, and wore dark glasses even when there was no sun. She was dressed in a habit, and had two shells hanging from her ears. — Please sit down — she told the man, as if they'd parted from each other only five minutes before. — I'm glad you came. The old fellow leaves me alone seven months in the year, which is just as well, for otherwise one would die of boredom. Just think, he doesn't even like staying in a convent.

The 'old fellow' was presumably her husband. But who had ever seen him? The man looked round. He found himself in the cloister of an ancient, dilapidated convent which the old Micky had had restored beside the villa where she now lived. Or rather where she was supposed to live, since for some time past everything had been happening in the convent, including parties and dinners. The refectory was a bit dark, but according to her 'it lifted up the heart'. They even slept there—that is, she and her friends—in certain bare rooms with chipped, brick floors. Each room had a huge dark Crucifix and wash basin. Half-hidden in the wall, there was a small door leading to a large, green-tiled bath-room. Everything else was suitably mouldy. In the ogival room into which the visitor had been shown, one could see a tall marble vessel for holy water. Every now and then a bell rang. — Do you hear? — Micky inquired — I've taken on a gardener who used to be a bell-ringer and who knows the canonical hours. Complines, matins. . . . He takes it all so seriously. The only trouble is that he rings the bell a bit too often. . . .

— But you don't know — she continued, introducing the man to her friends (who were like her in physical form and name: Freya, Cassandra, Violante), — you don't know that some years ago I would have married this man. Do you remember, Piffi? Then one day he told me: I'm too old for you. He was thirty-three and I was eighteen. What could I say? At the time I couldn't think what to say, so he left and I married Lucky. How funny! But he is a dangerous witness, you see. When I knew him, I used to believe in psychoanalysis. . . . And I thought that earthly love could make me happy.

There Freya, Cassandra and Violante all joined in a squeaky chorus of exclamation. Is it true Mike? How could such a thing happen? — I can't tell you how, but I will tell you exactly what happened. I've already explained to you that I jumped from the fourth to the seventh circle in a matter of a few years. It was a case of accelerated development. The man was at a loss. — Micky . . . Michelangiola. . . . What fourth circle are you talking about? The fourth circle of the moon?

Her friends look nonplussed. Michelangiola took it upon herself to offer excuses on his behalf.

— Please be patient. I don't think he knows anything about it. The fourth to the seventh circle of incarnation, you know; please try to understand. Don't you know anything about Karma? Absolute dark .And yet you yourself must be a fairly evolved type, not lower down than six, I should imagine. Perfection is a long laborious process. Many reach it by slow degrees, it's more or less like taking one's driving-test; you're told you need more lessons, that you don't corner well. Others fly through it, as I did, since it was my last incarnation.

An ill-shaven waiter entered, and made a sign to her. Michelangiola excused herself, got up and left with him.

Freya, Cassandra and Violante broke out in another chorus of squeaks. — Poor soul! The seventh circle! It's even worse than that if only one knew all she's had to go through! (The bell rang. Pause.)

And then Michelangiola came back.

— How do you get on with your servant, Piffi? — Micky asked — I used to have one, a rebellious type who used to discuss weird things. I'll spare you the details, since you haven't had your tea yet. But what sort of equality, exploitation, or rights, I used to ask him? What's the point of discussing such silly things if the whole problem is quite different? If you get so much out of so much, if you have worries and problems and bothers, it's only because your *Karma* is for the moment what it is. To expect more would be like wanting to extract blood from a stone. Wait your turn and you'll see what sort of fate the future has in store for you. They're all alike—these penniless people. They just won't wait and get angry with those who're flying or who have already flown.

Freya, the most masculine of all, intervened — But have you really killed him?

— Yes, of course — Michelangiola confirmed. — But if you think it leaves no traces, you're wrong. Poor child! You see, Piffi, the spirit is more sensitive than any membrane. Protest, my son, be sulky, I told him: you don't know what you're missing. . . . You don't know. . . .

The bell rang again. It was time to go to the refectory for tea.

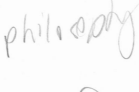

The Slow Club

Well, I've applied for membership of the Slow Club. A branch has recently been opened in our city. Among the details about myself that I've had to fill in for my application I had to state that I walk and that I possess neither a car nor a driving licence. In fact, the Club resists the 'wear and tear of modern times' not only by encouraging the use of herbal teas and medicaments, but also by recommending a decidedly anachronistic dress and way of life for its members.

The Club is situated in a vaguely palladian villa not far from the town. It has no telephone and its furnishings range from Tudor style to Biedermeier. It is heated by wood fires and the newspapers arrive some years late. This accounts for occasional bickering with the authorities and endless argument over prices which always seem unfavourable to the members.

The Secretary, while showing me round the rooms, drew my attention to the most recent portrait on the walls, that of the beautiful Otero, and told me that the most modern poet in the library was the glorious Baffo. In the reading room I admired an old Alsatian clock—one of those with a cuckoo.

In the bar only camomile tea and tangerine punch can be ordered. The games provided include draughts, tombola and cribbage, but not chess which requires too much brain work.

Women are not admitted to the Club, nor are talkative people. Even less welcome are those belonging to the proselitising professions: civil servants and priests.

In the course of my tour, as I paused to admire the beautiful bindings of *Scena illustrata*, I could hear the members talking in low subdued voices. Here are a few examples of what I overheard.

First member: Our fellow member, Wicker, of the Chicago branch, who is studying the vital rhythm of the snail, once told me that it could not compare with our own. If a snail managed to see a whole man, it wouldn't be able to gather anything about him, for it would be impossible for it to distinguish his sounds and movements. Wicker has sent his works to us by surface mail. In a couple of years we will be able to consult them in our library.

Second member: A relative of mine was married yesterday. You will receive the announcement in a few months' time. She got engaged in 1914, but, on hearing that her father was seriously wounded, took a vow before the Virgin that she would not marry until she had finished embroidering four hundred chasubles. When her father recovered and her fiancé returned safely from the Front, the girl refused to break her vow. Only a month ago the last chasuble was finished and so the fiancé, unconsciously re-enacting the beautiful story of Isaac, was able to lead her to the altar after thirty-three years of faithful waiting.

Third member: Some of you may remember my university friend, Carlo Marinelli. Just a few days after hearing from his young wife that she was expecting their first (and, as it turned out, their only) baby, he was killed at the gates of Gorizia in 1916. Carlo answered the letter at once, but as the irony of fate would have it, it was delivered only a few days ago, i.e. some thirty-one years after it was posted. You can imagine with what trepidation the widow, now grey-haired, recognised his handwriting. Among other things, including profuse expressions of affection, Carlo had asked her to name the child Marmaduke if it was a boy and Margaret if a girl. It was too late, for the child, now a wife and mother herself, had been named Ann. But as chance would have it, Ann was expecting another child, so it seemed as if after all Carlo's last wish was going to be satisfied after a lapse of a generation.

Fourth member: In a few days I'll be able to offer the members a china tea-set which I received some time ago. It was acquired in China in 1819 by Admiral Lonefield—an ancestor of my wife's. The Admiral, impressed by the skill of certain local craftsmen, ordered some cups and saucers to be painted. The factory manager agreed, 'but', he added, 'we don't under-

Factor Fiction

take mass-production—especially not for a customer like you. Give us some time, just a few years and you'll get the finest tea-set anyone has ever seen in England.' Sir Roger Lonefield was rather surprised, but he accepted the proposal, left a deposit, and set off for home. On his way back his boat, the *Green Bird*, foundered off the Liberian coast and there were no survivors. A month ago in January 1953, my wife, the last descendant of the Lonefields, received a large chest marked EXTREMELY FRAGILE. It contained pieces of porcelain, wrapped up in layers of cotton, leaves and mistletoe to render it shock-proof. Some of the pieces showed the Admiral's face, others his achievements. The experts think it's a miracle. We did not have to pay anything. The covering note explained that the sum paid by Sir Roger had earned enough interest in the past hundred and thirty-three years to cover the expense, even taking into account the inevitable devaluation of money. The letter also contained apologies for the slight delay caused by the company's search for the Lonefield heirs—a delay compensated for by the loving care and high artistic skill devoted by the best Chinese painters to the task.

I would have enjoyed listening longer but suspicious faces began to swivel round from the sofas in order to give the newcomer a closer look. The cuckoo poked its head out half a dozen times to strike the hours (cu-koo, cu-koo, cu-koo, cu-koo, cu-koo, cu-koo) marking time in the most exasperatingly measured fashion. They all got up saying 'It's getting late'.

'In a few years you'll hear the outcome of your application,' the Secretary said as he accompanied me out. 'As long as you keep out of the news, it is unlikely you will be blackballed. I have ordered a carriage for you.'

In fact, in front of the gate, a horse-drawn phaeton, with liveried coachmen, was waiting to take me back to the city.

Part III

The Bat

Just before midnight the man was going to turn off the light when a sinister shadow—a scrawl on the walls, a rapid zig-zag —flitted like lightning over his head, and disappeared towards the curtain that hid the wash-basin. Suddenly there was a piercing cry.

— A bat! — she shouted as she lay tossing about in terror. — What sort of hotel have you dragged me into? Get it out, for God's sake get it out!

She kept shouting, hidden under the sheet for fear of being contaminated by its filthy swooping. Her words were muffled and confused; she suggested he should chase it out with a stick, or with an umbrella, keeping the window wide open and the light turned off. Perhaps, attracted by the lights outside, who knows. . . .

With his head covered by a towel the man, in pyjamas, ran about in the dark, stumbling against the chairs, and brandishing a rolled-up magazine.

— The umbrella! — she shouted inarticulately (but there was no umbrella). At last, he touched a switch on the wall, causing a luminous wave to spurt from a transparent shell high above.

— It may have gone — he said, trying to look unconcerned; and went towards the window to close it. But suddenly something wriggling and sticky grazed his chest, flitting wildly around against the wall and then disappeared out of reach on top of a dark wardrobe. — Help, help! — the woman cried out, peering from the cushion which she had put over her head. Then, more calmly, not seeing the contortions on the wall — Has the monster gone? Say it's gone.

— I'm afraid not — he said, trying to soften the harsh truth (the shadow on the top of the wardrobe shook as if it were making renewed attempts at escape). — I'm afraid not, but I'll see that it does. Put your head down, don't panic.

He got up on a chair, covered his head again, and with a

well-aimed lob deposited the magazine on the top of the ward-robe; whereupon, amid a great cloud of dust and much erratic flying, the creature took off only to land struggling in the waste-paper basket.

— Help, help! — she yelled. Armed with a Moroccan slipper, and holding a rug before his eyes, the man advanced towards the wicker basket muttering — I'll take care of it; I'll turn the basket upside down and imprison it. Stop making a fuss.

When he thought he was near his target, though in fact he wasn't, he kicked the basket in an attempt to turn it upside down without spilling the contents. The basket rolled over, scattering egg-shells, ashes and used matches, while a shadow darted out towards the alabaster shell in which the ceiling lamp shone like a pearl in an oyster.

— Nothing to be done — he confessed, sitting on the edge of the bed. — It doesn't want to go. Don't be nervous. Let me rest and then I'll carry on.

— Ring the bell — she moaned from the depth of her smother-ing blankets. — Call the waitress—the Potiphar who opened the window. Let her deal with this vampire. . . .

— Be quiet, darling, we're not in Italy, no one would come at this time of night. But one could, now that I think of it, one could. . . .

— Ring the porter — implored the half-drowned voice. — Put something on your head and lie down here, only don't uncover me. Take the receiver and talk to him, since you know foreign languages.

— Languages! — he said, half-throttled by the carpet and groping towards the bed. — How does one say, how the devil does one say 'pipistrello' in another language? (From the floor below someone kept barking 'Hello, hello' into the receiver.)

— *Chauve-souris*, *pipistrello*, perhaps bat — she hissed in her muffled voice.

— Ah, those novels stand you in good stead — he grunted through the rug enveloping his head. Then, putting his mouth close to the receiver, he continued: — 'Hello, hello': *Chauve-souris, pipistrello*, perhaps bat. No, I'm not mad (he says I am), *Chauve-souris*, perhaps bat, in my room. Please come. Help! Help! Help! *Au secours*! Hello, hello! (Incomprehensible imprecations and strangled curses issued from the receiver and then there was the sound of someone putting it back.) — What did he say? — inquired the muffled voice.

— He's coming at once, no not at once, but he's coming . . . perhaps he's coming anyway. I don't know if he understood. But wait, darling, wait a little.

He rose to his feet with a courage and a decisiveness that surprised even himself. Throwing the carpet off he sat down in an armchair covered in floral chintz, the only chair in the room. The berserk shadow was still threshing about in the alabaster shell, so that the light was continually obliterated.

— Wait a moment — he went on — are you sure that *Pipistrello* means bat? Are you quite sure? Yes? Even that ass of a porter repeated the word 'bat', as if he knew it. Keep calm; he'll come with a broom — a broom, he must have used the word 'broom' — and put everything straight. But the Bat, wasn't that the name of the restaurant where we first met? I seem to remember the entrance being painted with huge black wings. . . .

— Yes, quite sure — her sobbing voice filtered up through the layers of quilt. — It was the 'Pipistrello', I'm sure it was.

— Strange — he said, keeping his eye on the shell. — Do you know that a bat is the only animal I've ever killed? They all said it was impossible to hit because of its erratic flight. One shot's quite enough to bring it down; just one hole in its sticky wings. But then who could do it? Who was capable of aiming that shot? They all fired—two, three, four of them, but nothing happened. Instead, other bats arrived, more and more of them. They seemed to be mocking us. Then I fired, almost at random; it was the first time I had ever used a revolver. The bat fell to the ground like a flabby handkerchief, twitched a little . . . and then died.

The sobbing increased.

Different message

— They're not ugly, you know? Actually they're like rats, with wings like cobwebs. They feed on mosquitoes and don't harm anyone. Unfortunately my bat wasn't dead, it kept hopping about like this one. But don't cry, another animal's coming, the porter. We'll have to give him two or three shillings; perhaps more, it depends on how long the chase lasts. Don't cry, it's not much. Now let me think: this is not even the second, but the third important bat in my life. The first you know, the second . . . is you, more or less, don't be offended; the third has dropped in this evening. And we welcome it by hurling glossy magazines, slippers and rugs at it. Soon, if it's not already dead, it'll be finished off with the broom. I don't know if that's fair. I really don't. No, don't cry. I'm only saying this for the sake of talking. Let's see what's to be done. The best thing would be to lift it gently and throw it out. If, for instance, it could be trapped in the waste-paper basket, we could then throw them both out of the window. Let me think. . . .

He threw himself on the bed, burrowing under the heaped blankets as far as he could reach — And supposing — he whispered into her ears — supposing it's my father come to visit me?

With a sharp cry she threw off everything—blankets, cushions, sheets—and sat bolt upright in the bed. The brooding spirit of the imprisoned bat no longer obsessed her.

— You're really crazy — she said, staring at his face. — Come, let's put something on and go down. They'll give us another room or we can walk for a couple of hours in the garden. There'll be no one about and it's not cold. I'll talk to the night porter. Your father? But why? A bat?

— I don't know — he said, almost on the verge of tears. — It's the only animal I've ever killed, with the exception, of course, of flies or ants. The only animal, and my father was very unhappy about it. I think he comes back sometimes to visit me in one form or another.—We'll meet again somewhere—he told me the day before he died.—You're too silly to be able to manage by yourself. Don't worry, I'll take care, I'll find ways and means of doing it.—But I'd almost forgotten it. Only now and then, when I see . . . one of these animals, take aim and *bang*! see it fall like a rag. It's then that the memory of him . . .

He aimed an imaginary gun in the direction of the bat and immediately something flew out, hit itself against the ceiling, disappeared through the window, and was swallowed up by the dark. With another shriek she threw herself back against the cushions. At that second there was a knock.

— It *would* be the porter — he said, hurrying over to close the window, and shouted — Just a minute, please, just a minute. — Then in an undertone — See if you've got half a crown, some silver, but not too much. After all, the fool hasn't done anything.

Having taken the coin, he opened the door, carrying on a subdued conversation for several minutes in the corridor. For her part, her eyes wide open, she kept looking where the bat had been, her mind on the restaurant with the black wings. Then, all of a sudden, remembering how years ago her life had been saved by her determination to see Strauss' *Pipistrello* —a bomb had destroyed her house in her absence—she had another wild outburst, before plunging back into the heap of blankets, laughing hysterically.

The Angiolino

In the dark room one suddenly hears an almost inaudible sound—a very faint whirr coming from the depth of a pigskin suitcase. To be able to hear it one has to be wide-awake and on the alert. A sigh, a yawn, a creaking of the bed, a stealthy footstep in'the corridor, is enough to suffocate the sound, and it dies away unheard. But that seldom happens. At half-past eight in the morning, even during the darkest days of winter, when every single person in the hotel is still immersed in sleep, he and she keep awake, waiting to be aroused by the small alarm clock called Angelo which they keep hidden in the suitcase. It's a square alarm clock, with a beautiful red case. If it were kept on the bedside table, it would glow because of its luminous phosphorus hands. But he can't stand the tick-tock of that mechanical little heart-like object and she doesn't like that bright aluminium face only two palms away from her. It creates an eerie feeling in the room, a *soupçon* as she calls it, to which she is not used. And anyway it's better to let time slip by without counting every second. The only solution is to bury the alarm-clock deep down in the suitcase and to stay awake, with eyes wide open, waiting to be called. It seldom happens that the alarm-clock rings without being heard, or finds them both asleep. He suffers from insomnia and she doesn't sleep well either. Then how could such an unlikely thing ever happen? They have a heated argument about it.

— Bad Angiolino — says the man, shaking the red leather case and holding it to his ear — Have you done it on purpose? Have you lost your voice? Or (turning frowningly to his wife) did you forget to wind it up?

— I've been winding it for twenty years, every evening at the same time. Sometimes I even get up twice in the night to check if I've wound it. It must have given the alarm while you were snoring. It has a very faint tone now, you know, as it's growing old. But if you're attentive, you can still hear it perfectly well. . . .

— I, snoring — he remonstrates, taking the electric razor from his chin — Don't you know that at four o'clock I'm always awake? It must have rung when those three negresses next door made all that racket. Haven't you ever heard them, the Paprika sisters? When they get back in the early hours it's every man for himself, for the whole building shakes.

— Last night they came in at four — she remarks, cleaning the face of the Angiolino with the hem of her night-gown — The child must have rung at nine o'clock. There's no earthly reason why it shouldn't.

Somebody knocks at the door; it's the waiter with two cups of coffee and a newspaper. There's a moment of silence. The waiter leaves and the two are left alone again. The man is moving the electric razor over the nape of his neck, producing an irritating buzz. Eventually, he unplugs the cord, stretches himself out on the bed and opens the paper. A few moments later, almost with a start:

— The child? — he asks — What child? It's idiotic to call this poor . . . alarm-clock that. Angiolino is not a child, it's an alarm-clock.

— It's you who said it was almost like our son. It's been travelling with us all these twenty years. I forbid you to insult him. (She takes the Angiolino, kisses it, puts it tenderly back in a little tartan bag and puts the bag in the leather case at the bottom of the suitcase.)

— That's quite enough — he bursts out in exasperation — Let's finish with these absurdities. No more of these spurious sons, these sentimentalities. It's high time we got down to brass tacks. Shall we try? Let's start this morning, let's start at once.

— All right — she says, with a sigh of resignation. But in the meantime the man, who is going through the newspaper, bursts into laughter. — You know — he tells her, stirring his *espresso* — Blackie Halligan, the hero of the Pacific, is dead; he was wounded several times and had a lot of medals. Do you know who he was? A carrier-pigeon that had saved the lives of three hundred men.

— What a good start for our pact — she points out — Aren't you going to tell me if war is going to break out, whether Cardinal Mindszenty was drugged or not? Why don't you explain what the Atlantic conscience means? I'm not interested in pigeons.

— Our pact can perfectly well start in half an hour, can't it? Oh hell! We've been telling each other such trivial things for thirty years now, we can't just stop like that, can we? You know even *they* don't take things so seriously, in spite of the fact they've won the war. Unfortunately, Italy has become a land of bureaucrats and pedants. We are all formalists, conservatives, ditherers, even in the most trivial matters. To attribute a human personality to a pigeon or even an alarm-clock is an innocent form of animism and animism is the most sensible and most logical spiritual position a man can adopt. For man can't get out of himself and can't measure things with any other rod but his own.

He's not quite happy about shaving against the lie of the hair, and has had to reattach the razor to the wall-plug, while she is absorbed in reading a foreign magazine. She raises her head to ask:

— What does high-brow mean? This paper says that there are millions of people in America who read books, but only twenty-five thousand are high-brows.

— Let me think. It means supercilious, readers whose taste it's difficult to satisfy, *emunctae naris*. What do they want to do with them? Shoot them?

— No, on the contrary, they're trying to increase them. They want at least one per cent of the population to be high-brow. That would mean even minority or learned books, those without gimmicks or murders, would have a million and a half readers. And ninety per cent of Americans would continue to read the usual books. It would be a heaven for all.

— And if we — he observes, slicking his cheeks —- if we had

been the high-brows of life, rather than of art? You read nothing but useless reviews, and nowadays I only read detective stories. But in life . . . in life everything's different. Angiolinos in the suitcase and prodigious pigeons in the sky—that's what we need.

— We? — she remarks with a certain bitterness — Speak for yourself. I did my best to toughen you against life. We're faced with terrible times. The Angelo . . . has been something very personal for me, a private flirtation. I should have helped you get used to the Roskoff—the sort of alarm-clock that looks like a steam-roller. Look, you must be a strong man, a very strong man, if you want to be taken seriously.

An almost imperceptible sound can be heard coming from the bottom of the suitcase—and lasts just a few seconds. He jumps out of bed and both of them in a state of great excitement burrow for the silk bag. Then they lift the alarm-clock, shake it, caress it and give it long loving looks.

— There's nothing wrong with it — he says, feeling ashamed about the change in his voice.—It was set for a quarter past nine, not nine. The small hand had slipped on a bit. From tonight on, if you don't mind, I'll wind up the alarm-clock myself.

He moves back in front of the mirror to reassure himself about his shave, and turning back, stammers: — Supposing our agreement were to start tomorrow?

Without saying a word, she nods her approval. She's putting the Angiolino back in the suitcase.

futuristic philosophy

The Relics

— I can't find the photo of Ortello — said the sick woman as she nervously rummaged in the box where she kept newspaper cuttings, old letters tied up with a ribbon, and some holy pictures which she dared not destroy (for one never knows . . .)
— Of course, you won't even remember who it was.
— It's (or was, if it's dead), a horse, a beautiful horse that won the Grand Prix at Longchamp. Of course, I remember it. Its photo was there I'm sure. You had never seen it race, but it had been your passion for ages. And so it ended up in your private reliquary. But now it seems to have taken flight. It was a piece of paper, and so it could have blown away.
— Ah — she said, tidying her hair which was the colour of a dry leaf. — You talk of *my* reliquary as if it were only my mania. Naturally, that's just what one would have expected. I suppose the wind's blown away something else too.
— The Okapi? — asked the bald man with a start. — Impossible, look more carefully.
— Exactly, the Okapi, that weird animal, half goat, half pig, whose memory you wanted to perpetuate. It's flown away with the horse. You've quite a good memory for the things that interest you.
— Half pig? — he asked animatedly. — Say half donkey, half zebra, half gazelle, and half angel. A unique specimen, belonging to a species said to have been extinct for centuries. I wanted to go to London just to see it at the zoo. It trembles nervously the moment it sees a man: it's too sensitive to be among wild animals like us. I wonder if they've been able to keep it alive. There's no question of finding a male for it. It's unique, you know, unique.
— Lucky fellow — was the answer, which was meant to be a reprimand.
They kept quiet for a while. She was lying in an arm-chair and looking at the allegorical scenes painted on the ceiling—

scenes depicting animals and gods, but not the sort of animals and gods she could feel at home with. He was looking through the window-panes at the top of a wind-ruffled poplar. Further away one could see the already snow-covered slopes of the Alps. It had started raining and the panes were soon furrowed by rain drops. It was beginning to get dark, and the nymphs and swans on the ceiling would soon be blotted out. They realised this only when the waitress came in with the tea and flicked the switch of the chandelier. A soft light suffused the fake antiques. And even the sound of the rain became more cheerful.

— Oh, a bit of light — he said, as he helped her wrap herself up in her shawl. — One can't talk properly in the dark. One doesn't often realise it, but having some light even helps to clear up ideas. You're in a bad mood today.

— No. I'm simply making a list of our souvenirs, the only thread that still holds us together after all this time. In the meantime the ones in the box have gone, I don't know whether through your carelessness or mine. But so many others must be lying locked up in my mind, that are not to be found in yours, if I'm to judge by your coldness, by your marmot's silence.

— I, a marmot? — he protested as he smoothed down the spikes of his glossy head. — As for marmots, you might have thought of something better. Well, where did we see one?

— Near San Galgano abbey; a hunter had a few of them; you remember he offered to sell us his own son, a beautiful pink and white creature, a babe in arms. He told his wife that he meant it, for, after all, what did it matter? He would soon have brought about another. But we didn't take the son; it would have cost us too much . . . to maintain him.

— I congratulate you on your good memory. That was only a marten; and it was dead. The martens, the three martens . . .

— We saw them in a small cave on the huge crag with the Gornergrat funicular passing over. They were dancing happily about, waving their paws and greeting the travellers. They felt quite safe. But there weren't three; there was a whole family, father, mother, children. Milk or lemon?

— Neither, thank you — he said as he took the cup. Then he looked round. The waitress had left. After a pause he asked, with studied nonchalance: — And . . . the fox?

— The red fox, you mean? At first she went into her little den in the cage, at Zermatt. She didn't want to be seen. I said to myself: I'll count twenty, and if she comes out in the meantime then what's to happen will happen and if she doesn't . . . then this man can go to the devil! And so I counted slowly, more and more slowly. At nineteen the fox came out.

— And so you decided to marry me — he said, waiting for his tea to cool. — I see, I see. One never stops learning.

— Don't complain, I deliberately counted slowly. Perhaps after nineteen I would have made an extra long pause. It was I who brought the fox out . . . with my wish. Of course, one had to play a kind of game. I had to slacken the tempo. Like certain musicians.

— Well, since we're in a confessing mood, I'll admit that when Mimì was about to re-enter the box, at Vitznau, I told myself: if it enters the box on the right, then what's going to happen will happen; but if it enters the one on the left, then. . . . You know what I mean. Mimì, the white and yellow guinea-pig. Don't you remember?

— Perfectly well. And Mimì, having come out of the conjuror's sleeve, ended up in the right-hand box? That means that our union has a very solid basis. Do you want a biscuit?

— No, thanks. It ended up in the left-hand one. But the experiment was repeated three times, and you won two to one; which was enough. There was no trick, you see.

— The fox and the guinea-pig, two interesting godfathers. They must have died long ago without having ever realised what a mess they had been responsible for. Our life is a bestiary, a menagerie in fact. Do you think you've thrown them away? Cats, dogs, birds, blackbirds, turtle-doves, crickets, worms. . . .

— Oh worms — he said, contemptuously.

— ... even worms, and I don't know what else. And the names? Buck Pallino Passepoil Pippo Bubù. . . .

— Lapo Esmeralda Mascotto Pinco Tartufo Margot. . . .

He went on, at times even inventing a name, but then he stopped, noticing that she had closed her eyes, exhausted. He took a dry biscuit from the plate and put it into his mouth. Then he instinctively stretched his hand towards the cardboard box and started ransacking among the cuttings, photographs, old letters. From a seemingly empty envelope two rumpled photos came out: a highly strung, fine looking colt and a curious animal with a wandering eye, that seemed to oscillate between a Bedlington and a badger, a sucking-pig and a roe-buck, a goat and a small Pantellerian donkey; perhaps a blunder, a misprint on the part of the great Foreman, but nevertheless a joy to the eye, an indescribable hope for the heart. — The Ocapi! Ortello! — he exclaimed as he smote his head. — I've found it! I've found both!

But she had fallen asleep. Outside it had stopped raining, or almost. He put the cuttings gently on her folded hands and said to himself: I'll go out for a walk, but won't turn off the light. When she wakes up, she'll see them at once.

And he stole quietly away from the room.

The Russian Prince

Au pied de Porc — Carlo said to the driver—and when asked to give further details, he added in bad French: — It's a road intersecting Rue de l'Odéon; I'll point it out when we get there.

The driver set off, with no particular enthusiasm. He was a grey-haired man, with a moustache, and was wearing a peaked cap. But the eyes . . . — Have you noticed his eyes? — Adelina asked — They're like the sea, absolutely marvellous. He must be a Russian nobleman, perhaps a prince.

— A Russian? But why on earth a Russian? And in any case how could you tell?

— There are one thousand five hundred taxi drivers in Paris, almost all descendants of the nobility. Please give him a good tip. We really ought to be talking to him out of politeness. And turning to the taxi driver, who had his foot down on the accelerator:

— It's rather warm, Monsieur, isn't it?

— *Bien sûr Madame* — the so-called prince grunted, swerving and narrowly avoiding a careless cyclist.

— He doesn't want to talk — Carlo said — Let him drive in peace.

— He's quite a nice man, I could see that at once. Do you think fifty francs would do? It's a bit embarassing, because one doesn't want to offend him.

Rue de l'Odéon was in sight, but Carlo, who was looking out of the window, couldn't see anything resembling the *Pied de Porc*, whose whereabouts he knew only vaguely. Slowing down, the taxi driver looked back inquiringly.

— More to the other side . . . a bit further up . . . perhaps on the right . . . no, turn left . . . — Carlo directed, but there was no trace anywhere of a sign-board with a pig's snout on it. The taxi driver began grumbling, looking more and more sullen.

— You are making a hash of it! — Adelina murmured — You
have to have a lot of patience. Thank goodness the taxi-driver's
a real gentleman.

— He's a real rogue — Carlo answered. — After all he'll get
what's on the meter. The car zig-zagged through several streets,
turned back and then went up all the intersections and side-
streets. All in vain. At a certain point the taxi-driver got out
of the taxi, and went up to ask a group of workers standing
at a corner. Then he got in again and started off with the
air of a man saying to himself: 'Now I know where it is.'

He drove for another half mile, entered a dark, deserted
lane, and stopped in front of a sign-board on which one could
make out the words *Au pied de cochon.*

— Voilà le porc — he said, turning his head.

— This is not it — Carlo fumed. — The description I was
given of the place was quite different: a small tree-lined square,
a shop-window with oysters, pheasants and partridges. And
then it's *porc*, not *cochon.* — And turning to the taxi-driver:
— *Je cherche le porc, pas du tout le cochon.*

— *Eh bien, Monsieur* — said the taxi-driver, opening the door.
— *C'est bien la même chose: c'est toujours de la cochonnerie.*

Carlo wanted to answer back but Adelina restrained him.
They got down, paid 320 old francs, Adelina adding another
fifty francs, and the taxi-driver drove off. They said goodbye
as he left, but he didn't answer.

— What a *rustre*! — Carlo complained putting the change in
his pocket. — He put us down where *he* wanted to.

— All the same, that was a good joke: *c'est toujours de la cochonnerie.* What Italian or French taxi-driver would be able to
say such a thing? I'm sure he's a Russian aristocrat. What
else could you expect from him? That he should know by
heart every Parisian *gargotte*? You ought to have given him a
more accurate address.

— What Russian! He's a rogue from the Camargue, a drunken
lout.

— And you're an idiot.

121

— And you're a bloody little fool!
— Well, I'm not going to eat anything now.
— Nor am I.

Without noticing it, they had sat down at a small table. The *trattoria* was gloomy, empty, perhaps even very expensive. A waiter produced the menu, suggesting: *Hors d'oeuvre? Escargots?*

Crying all the time, she said yes, she was going to eat snails.

'Would you like to
change yourself into ...?'

Since the early hours of the morning (that's to say, the early
hours for the bathers, ten or eleven o'clock) they've been
wandering around in the pine-woods and on the beach. They
gaze, peer, listen, and every now and then make a note in a
small pocket book. But their busiest time is the late afternoon,
when people gather together, talk and confide in each other,
revealing their secrets (if any).
— Would you like to change yourself into him? — Frika
asks Alberico, pointing to a hairy lawyer in shorts, who is
playing at cards. Her attention was drawn to him because of
his loud confident voice, riding the breeze.
— I? Of course, at once — Alberico answers and makes a
mark in the diary.
A woman walks by in the scantiest of bathing costumes,
bra, briefs and golden sandals. She's like a beautiful statue—red
and blonde. Every year she comes from Busto by car, together
with a child and a governess.
— Would you like to change yourself into her? — Alberico
asks. And Frika:
— What a question! Without the least hesitation — and she
too makes a little mark in the diary.
Then an old woman wanders on to the beach. She has
bleached hair, and is carrying a white poodle in her arms, all
hairy from the stomach upwards and clean-shaven from the
stomach downwards: a ball of fluff, half bald, half shaggy,
showing clear patches of pink flea-ridden skin and looking
around with its little dark eyes. — Come on Cheap, my
darling — the old woman says, adding that Cheap is like a son
to her, but that she wouldn't want one again, as it gives her
so much bother. But then what can one do? Anyway now
that it's there, she never lets it feel the lack of anything. Poor

Cheap, how it cries and despairs the moment she's away. It suffers from a liver complaint, but is still going strong and might live another ten years. Come, my darling, come to your mother.

— Would you like to change yourself . . .? Frika inquires.

— Into her? — Alberico asks in amazement.

— No, into Cheap.

— Straight away — Alberico replies and makes a note in the diary.

— I, too, into her — Frika agrees. — Yes even into her, for at least she has her Cheap — And she, in her turn, makes a note or two.

They have reached the corner where the cobbler works in the dark shadow of dusty ilexes. She gives him her sandal and he bends over it and starts mending it. A slow, sweet, rather melancholy singing drifts down to them.

— It's a titmouse — the cobbler says — It's been singing for years. But I've never been able to set eyes on it — the last beautiful thing left on earth, I imagine.

They listen with rapt attention. Alberico makes a mark in the diary.

— Into the cobbler? — she whispers.

— No, into the titmouse — he says — but come to think of it, why not? — and he makes another note.

She also nods, but makes only one mark—for the titmouse.

So many years have passed since they were married; perhaps the only thing that has kept them together are the Wagnerian names. But it's too late now. And so they keep playing this game for hours on end, wherever they happen to be, on boats, on the beach, in bed, in deck-chairs. And at night they add it all up to see who has got the most points, which one is unhappier than the other, and who is more disposed to *change himself into another person. . . .*

A Difficult Evening

The very first day when, in a moment of tenderness, he called her—who knows why?—a 'pantegana', his beloved 'pantegana', she wasn't at all suspicious. — Pantegana? What's that? An animal, a toad, a flower? — Yes — he replied — an animal, but not really an animal: a charming little furry object, a kind of ferret or weasel or chinchilla. . . .

But that evening, no sooner had the gondola left the Rialto bridge and entered a dark canal, than it was rocked by a splash. She raised her face from between her hands and asked: 'What's that?' 'It's a pantegana,' the gondolier answered, and the whole drama unfolded itself in a few seconds.

— It's a mouse — she said, her eyes wide open, and staring at some ripples in the dirty water of the canal. It's a filthy water-rat. And you had the nerve. . . .

— I? — he murmured, having sensed the coming storm. — A rat? What on earth are you talking about? Look carefully (the ripples were drifting farther and farther away), it can't be a rat; it's more like an otter, a beaver, with such lovely fur.

The ripple had disappeared, but then a stronger splash was heard and when the gondola passed a small shrine with the candles burning round the statue of the Madonna, she could see a pantegana crossing the water—half-submerged, slimy and swollen, with its long obscene tail twisted like a cork-screw, its muzzle protruding from sawdust and floating lemon peel, its dirty eyes, its long dripping moustaches, and its tiny claws scrabbling frantically among the garbage.

— The pantegana! How horrible! — she was crying — Let me have a better look!

He gestured to the gondolier, to urge him on. But he had already turned, and the creature was barely a foot away. For a moment it was completely dark. Then a beam of light from a window illuminated the patch where the animal was scuffling. She leaned forward, peering short-sightedly at it.

— Are my eyes like those? — she was sobbing hysterically — Have I got those moustaches? Is my hair that filthy colour?

— Of course not, Signora — the gondolier broke in, the other still pleading desperately: — Can't you see it's a joke, the Venetian 'pantegane' are something quite different. They're these revolting rats; but the other ones. . . .

He stopped; she'd calmed down. The 'pantegana' had leapt out of the water and disappeared down a drain. The gondola was gliding along and they could make out the Bridge of Sighs a few yards away. She was still sobbing.

— Of course — the man went on nervously — here, in these sewers. . . . But you see, in other places, where the water . . .

She gave him an icy look.

— As soon as we get to the hotel, please call a motor-boat — she snapped — I'm leaving tonight. I'll write to you later and let you know where to send on my luggage.

The Red Mushrooms

Late in the evening they used to assemble in an empty back-shop and discuss various ways of celebrating the fall (and preferably the death) of the tyrant. And since all three or four of them were gluttons, or at least *gourmets*, the imagined saturnalias always took the form of rich and sumptuous dinners. They had no political ambitions. Moreover, the eventuality of the rascal's collapse was so unpredictable that it would have been really rather absurd to think in terms of loot.

— When 'he' dies — Abela muttered in a low voice (the walls have ears, you know) — we shall eat rice *alla valenzana*, snails *alla bordolese*, and a *soufflet al vieux Prunier*. It will be on me, naturally. I shall get hold of the best cook in town.

— If someone could only kill him — mumbled Egisto, looking round suspiciously — I'd prepare for all of you a soup of crayfish claws that not even the Heavenly Father has ever eaten. And as to the wines, yes, as to the wines, I have down in the cellar . . .

— If he gets an apoplectic fit — Volfango interrupted loudly (only someone put a hand over his mouth to gag him) — I'll prepare *cappelletti* as I alone know how to do it, followed by a pig cooked on the spit, a well-roasted suckling, and then down in the cellar a river of Lambrusco . . .

— When he pops off — Ferruccio exclaimed, jumping breathlessly to his feet with eyes rolling — we'll need something better than that! A single dish—one of those dishes that make you mad, a roe-buck stew, and with that. . .

— With what? — the other three demanded.

— With that, fried red mushrooms, washed down with a white Verdicchio, half a potato, half a tomato, a stick of celery, a pinch of ginger, a drop of rum, a sprinkling of fennel, and then . . . after half an hour's slow cooking, a light skim of cream, a drop, just a mere notion, of Modena vinegar; and last of all . . .

— And last of all? — Abele, Egisto and Volfango asked eagerly together.

— And last of all . . . it's not finished yet . . . and last of all . . .

He searched for it in his memory, groped about in the air, staggered. They rushed to him just in time to prevent him from falling and laid him on the sofa. He had gone very pale and it looked as if he had stopped breathing. Abele felt his pulse and shook his head.

— We must ring for an ambulance at once — he said. — As far as I'm concerned, he's a goner. I knew this might happen. No good comes from this kind of talk.

The Ash

The pontoon-bridge leading to the top of the slope, right in front of the Isoletto dell'Indiano, was not far off, but unfortunately it was inaccessible to the public. A short while before, some important people had passed by, wrapped in dark cloaks, to the meagre applause and obsequious greetings of officials who lit their way with smoky torches and pocket lamps aimed like revolvers. The bridge was in the process of being dismantled to keep the crowd out. Beams from powerful reflectors probed the sky and the vast mob surging round the Isoletto was blinded by huge revolving lights. Producers armed with megaphones and whistles, telephonists, linesmen, special correspondents and other staff bustled about all over the place.

As I approached the pontoon, I must have made somebody suspicious, for one of the fire-men approached me. He pointed a torch between my eyes. It was spurting an unpleasant blue light.

— Identity-card — he drawled. He peered into it to check whether I really resembled my photograph. — Clear out of here — he ordered at length, indicating a slope down which one could reach the parapet along the river.

Soon afterwards I found myself standing by a wall under a pale lantern, somewhat away from the crowd and bridge. Beside me a red-haired woman was engrossed in watching a snail's progress over the wall. She must have been thirty, perhaps thirty-five, and the man with her, who had just lit a huge Minghetti cigar, seemed younger. They were talking animatedly, but the roar of aeroplanes passing low overhead prevented me from catching their words. The show on the island had begun—a motorised and aerial spectacle for thousands of spectators which, according to the press, was finally going to supersede the bourgeois theatre.

I couldn't really make out what was happening over on the

island, so I remained sitting on the wall, lost in my own thoughts, until some noise or other made me look up. Down below, among the trees and bushes, a table was being laid in the form of a horse-shoe. The word PARLAMENTO seemed to be written on it in huge letters. All the lights converged on the table and the diners seemed about to be flattened by an invasion of tanks sallying out of the dark with the apparent object of depositing them in the Arno.

— It's stuck — she said, scarcely looking at it, her attention fixed on the snail that had crawled as far as the middle of the road, between the two parapets.

— Yes, it is — the man replied, huge puffs coming from his Minghetti cigar.

The table was in fact blocked by some invisible obstacle and the tanks that had knocked it down couldn't push it into the river. There was shouting and laughter all around. In the meantime the Social-Democrat guzzlers, tiny as ants, scattered in all directions, pursued by the tanks. A searchlight went out and the entertainment seemed to flag for the moment. But more aeroplanes flew over, the beam came on again, and further spectacular scenes were shown to the accompaniment of pipes and drums.

— I can't see why . . . — the red-haired woman commented peevishly, but she stopped short, since the tiny snail, with its white shell shining in the lamp-light, had stopped too.

— It's not the first time you've mentioned it — the man observed, puffing like a steam-engine.

For the sake of safety, he shuffled two steps to the right. The sky became overcast and it looked as if it might rain. Some frogs began to mingle their throaty croaking with the noises coming from the island. Huge ploughs and agricultural machines were seen tilling under spotlights the once sterile soil of the Empire, from which, as if in obedience to the producers' orders, spouted luminous ears of corn, cotton, rivers of oil running into capacious pipelines, lush orchards and spurious Russian dancers. The screeching sound of sirens could be heard and Bengal-lights spurted on the horizon. The noise of the crowd had subsided and soon, one by one, the floodlights began to fail. I returned to where I'd been standing.

— What's happening down there? — she asked in a calmer voice, pointing towards the island. She gazed down at the snail which had resumed its slobbery crawl over the wall.

— I think the League of Nations is on fire — he said, consulting the programme and puffing out smoke. He observed, with some satisfaction, the white ash from his cigar, which had formed a kind of cylinder not yet quite ready to disintegrate.

— Let it stay — she said — I've an idea.

The wind was getting up, the island was scoured by a confusion of lights and shadows. Coming from the streets along the banks of the Arno one could hear the sound of horns warning off passers-by. The crowds began to disperse in a mad stampede. Two men, accompanied by a police officer, hurried past us. They seemed to have come from the bridge.

— There's no discipline — one of them complained — it's been a complete fiasco. There's going to be trouble, you know. Galeazzo was fed up, too.

— What's your idea? — the young man with the cigar inquired, about to take his hat from the parapet.

— Just an idea, a little private idea of mine. Don't move.

An aeroplane skimmed low over them, creating an infernal din and causing havoc among the thousands of spectators. Suddenly my attention was attracted by a cry and I saw the red-haired woman cling round the man's neck and burst into convulsive sobbing. The ash from the Minghetti had dropped off and the cigar was burning brightly. The snail was no longer there.

— It's gone — she said, holding fast to him — it's gone. It took only half a second, but it had already gone over the other side of the parapet. . . .

— Half a second? It's gone? What on earth are you talking about? — the man repeated in bewilderment. And he looked at me as if he needed my help. She couldn't say a word for sobbing.

— Forgive me — I intervened. — The snail had actually gone over the other side of the parapet *before the ash of your cigar had fallen,* that's all. . . .

— Oh, really? Did it? . . . What do you mean exactly?

— That, I'm afraid, is what I can't tell you. But one can assume that the lady had come to attach a special significance to what I've just confirmed. Something in the nature of a vow or an omen. . . . Perhaps it had something to do with you?

The woman, half-smiling, half-confused, nodded her assent, and then went on sobbing, still clutching him.

The man with the cigar seemed more confused than ever, but he tried to console her. Then he turned to me:

— Excuse me, but how did *you* come to know all this? Do you read cards? Are you a conjurer?

— Something even worse, actually. I'm a journalist.

They went off, walking beside the parapet and turning back from time to time to look at me. I followed them at my own pace, having no desire for further parades or festivities. There was a fearful racket of traffic and people. The first cars must already have reached the Viale dei Colli, swept in the distance by beams of pinkish light.

The Producer

Almost submerged in the early morning fog, and with a sort of halo around him, the man who resembled Amerigo was standing on the footpath, looking at me. I withheld any sign of greeting, but smiled faintly, which he couldn't help noticing. — And so you recognise me? — he said. — Yes, it's me, Amerigo. ('Damn!' I said to myself. 'How is it that I thought he was dead? Some false rumour, one of those stupid bits of gossip that one accepts without checking. Thank goodness he knows nothing about it. . . .')

— How are you? — Amerigo went on — I was looking for you, along with some others. I happen to be here for a few days. I shouldn't tell you why, because it's confidential, only I haven't forgotten what you did for me that June in Vallarsa, when you sent me off on leave just before the offensive. I know you didn't want to save my skin; in fact you didn't like me; but precisely because of your unreasonable dislike for me you wanted to be a hundred per cent fair. So I owe you my life, and my first meeting with Y.,—the best bit of luck I've ever had—which took place during that leave. Don't thank me, just listen carefully (and above all keep it to yourself). We're making a film of the next fifty centuries which will be seen, or rather lived, by those actually concerned—each in turn and according to the parts they've played. Since you are still alive, you belong to the last film; no, no, not at all a bad film, don't worry, but certainly a rather old-fashioned one . . . too many close-ups, too many tracking shots, too many film stars. Now the story-line will be much more coherent, much more straightforward. And what music, as you'll soon hear! Strong as gun-fire and delicate as the whistling of a thrush. Of course, up there one always keeps abreast of the times, one's always up to date. In fact, we have a choice that you don't have.

— Of course — I stammered, leaning against a wall covered

with posters advertising road safety.—Of course, I understand
perfectly well, up there . . . of course, it's natural, a choice . . .
lot of choice, a very rich choice. . . . (The poster against which
I was leaning bore the inscription: 'Life is short, don't shorten
it further.')

— Now — he continued — it's not a question of offering you
a new part; actually, your part is almost over, and it's not been
a particularly brilliant one. Of course, I realise, it was not
your fault. In your time, stars were the thing and you weren't
born for this kind of rôle. You would have done better in the
new film, but, as I said, there's nothing to be done about it
now. You were born too soon. But don't worry. I can fix
you up with something in the new film, a part that exists in
the memory of the new actors. You're a writer, or you used
to be one, if I remember rightly. But don't hope for too much,
you can't—from what I hear—expect to be someone like
Homer. And I don't think that even immortality like Calli-
machus's—two hundred readers a century, and what readers!
—can be allotted to you either. Survival based on the merit
of your works I don't think I can grant you. Maybe you
deserve it. But what can one do? Information is information.
One can't be certain that the compilers aren't all imbeciles,
but one can't exactly throw them into the wastepaper basket
either. The new film reorganises and reassesses the data of the
old one; we can't make a clean sweep of everything. Maybe
we shall be able to do so one day, but for the moment we must
be content with things as they are. I myself would soon be
replaced by other producers, much worse than myself. So
what would you say if I gave you a subsidiary lead? No one
would read you in the new film, but you would be remembered
as someone who was once alive, as someone who lived in other
times. Would you like to become a character in a libretto,
only a minor character, naturally, someone like Angelotti
in *Tosca*? I think he really existed. Or would you prefer to have
your name associated with a beefsteak, like M. Chateaubriand?
Or perhaps you'd like your name to be given to a brooch, a

tie, a hair style or a new sub-species of dog. I know you used to have a soft spot for mongrels, we could pick on one and call it after you. But we must decide soon. I'm very busy and if I hadn't met you accidentally I'm not sure if I could have fitted you into my programme at all. Could you give me an idea, a hint?

I hesitated, taking a few steps in the fog, Amerigo trying to coax me. A green light behind me turned red and a line of motor cars seemed to swoop down on me, only to come to an abrupt halt at the sound of a whistle. A policeman in a dark raincoat came running towards me. — You've broken traffic regulations — he shouted. — Get away from there and join me on the island.

— Has he . . . traffic regulations, as well? — I inquired, looking at Amerigo who had already jumped to safety.

— He? Who are you talking about? — the policeman demanded, taking out a note-book. — Are you drunk or something?

Obviously he couldn't see anyone in the fog, but I could still make out the face that had smiled at me in Vallarsa more than thirty years ago.

ghost supernatural

The Widows

My best friends are all dead. Their wives, neither younger, better, nor more fit to be alive than they, are still there. They perpetuate their memory, are always in mourning, with ribbons and frills. They are complimented by dignitaries; preside over meetings; cut the thread at the opening of exhibitions, break bottles of champagne at launchings, correct the proofs of their late husbands' books, distribute scholarships, and one way and another keep wicks burning which for want of oil would rather be extinguished.

'Leave us in peace' the feeble voices of the dead sigh from underground. But the widows insist. And when the first shades of oblivion loom over the tea-tables spread out among the pines, in sight of the Appenines, they bend over the canasta and say: 'Stand back! *non praevalebunt.*'

These dear widows have now left the cities, and are scattered all over the sea-side and the mountains, watching through their binoculars, Alpinists climb Mount Cervino, floating like whales on the calm waters of the Lido, and eating *goulash* at the Cinquale's Hungarian bathing-hut, recognising one another by their smell and small talk . . . small talk about those who have preceded them to the Kingdom of Heaven. They are globe-trotters, worldly, haughty, snobbish, aloof. If they remarry, they still follow the cult of their *first.*

'Mein Mann,' says one; 'mon mari' says another; 'my husband' repeats a third. And a fourth whispers into the ears of a fifth: 'even at those particular times . . . you know, he liked me to keep my stockings on. . . .'

My best friends are all dead. I alone survive and fight against their cult as professed by their widows. I remember them in my own way—getting into a tram or sipping an apéritif, or at the sight of a dog's muzzle, the outline of a palm-tree, the parabola of a firework. Sometimes I come across them in the refuse which the sea carries away towards Calambrone, in the dregs of a glass of old Barolo, in a cat's leap as it chases a butterfly in a square at Massa. There's no voice to say 'My husband' and they're quite at home with me.

The Culprit

It was three o'clock in the afternoon. Federigo had got back to his office a few minutes before. Standing at a reading-desk which reached up to his neck, he started answering the letter from a stranger living in the distant town of Seattle (State of Washington), who had written to ask if Fruscoli the chiropodist was still to be found, where he used to live twenty years ago, in Via del Ronco. As a matter of fact, Federigo's was not an information bureau, but an Institute for popular culture which used to lend English, American and Italian books on all sorts of subjects, from theosophy to detective fiction. It was an old public Institute which had managed to survive for almost a century without being noticed by the authorities. Over the last few years, however, the 'officials' of the place had decided to take it under their protection and turn it into a semi-public, semi-private institute, something hard to describe and even harder to run. Unaffected by new fashions, Federigo continued to answer letters from strangers in Seattle or elsewhere, and thus kept alive the tradition of courtesy that had been practised within the four walls of the Institute for a long time.

Federigo used to work standing up! In the office (a narrow, high-ceilinged old chapel that was perishingly cold, a real hovel) there was no furniture other than the reading desk, the letter-press and some packets of papers. Scribbling away in front of Federigo, on the other side of the reading desk, was an old clerk with a cap on, an honest man, with a pug-nose, who was both the accountant and the organiser of the place. One could see the Institute itself through the glass of the chapel, a building like the nave of a church, with large stained-glass windows, curtains and book-cases reaching half way up the walls. On one side there was another old fellow in a cap, who was always gesticulating and almost always drunk. He was in charge of distribution and had a couple of shop-assistants under him. But on that particular afternoon almost no one turned up, except the usual blind eighty-year-old crone who used to be conducted by someone as far as the bench, where she would pronounce just one word 'Murder!', slip the latest detective novel into her bag, and disappear with a Roman salute.

It was about three o'clock, when all of a sudden—something quite unusual—the telephone rang on the damp ground floor, accessible through the hall of the decrepit Institute. Federigo hurried down and took the call. He registered a few dry words to the effect that Count Penzolini was waiting for him.

Federigo put on a dusty overcoat, wrapped a muffler round his neck, and within a few seconds was to be seen crossing the medieval square with its huge tower and palace. The unexpected telephone call had not upset him. He had no prophetic powers and was not one of those who let the grass grow under their feet or who anticipate disaster.

He entered the lift, paying out a *soldo* (his position entitled him to a discount of seventy-five per cent) and soon found himself in the Count's underfurnished but well-heated ante-room. Standing by a window, two men-servants, in white socks and livery, were throwing crumbs of bread through a small opening to a few pigeons outside in the cold. When Federigo informed them he had an appointment with the Count, they told him they were busy and went on with what they were doing. At length, one of them went away, telling Federigo to wait his turn.

There was nobody else waiting. Nor did any word come from the Count's office. Nevertheless, he had to wait his turn for about two hours. The servants went on throwing crumbs to the pigeons from the window-sill. Now and then one of the staff would pass through with a paper in his hand. Scarcely a sound reached him from the traffic in the piazza. On the other side of the glass a landscape of bell-towers and spires suffused by the sunset soothed Federigo's myopic eyes. It must have been five o'clock before he heard people talking in the next room. Perhaps the Count had come to his office? Then a servant, even more dolled up than the others, informed Federigo curtly — It's your turn. You can go in.

As Federigo entered, he almost slipped over on the polished tiles of the Count's large but quite unpretentious office. There were no papers lying about on the table, a practice quite modish at that time. Instead, the portraits of important people hung from the walls, and beside the window, on a tripod, there stood an ebony relief which, from whatever side one looked at it, reproduced the imperious profile of the only Man to whom, in those years, belonged the honour of the ritual capital letter. It was, in fact, a historical mask of His, devised in conformity with a patented mould that had become very popular.

Count Penzolini was standing before his office table. He seemed to be about forty, tall, clean shaven, with grey, fishy eyes, and some distinctive badges on his collar. A piece of paper fixed on the wall bore the words: 'Brief visits'; and another one: 'It is not necessary to live,' etc. A third one contained a longer, probably more ominous, phrase which Federigo hadn't been able to decipher. The Count raised an arm and the visitor followed suit as best he could.

— You wanted to see me, Signor Conte? — Federigo asked nervously. He didn't know why, but he was already feeling uncomfortable.

— Please sit down — the Count said. He opened a drawer, took out a sheet of paper and started reading it. Then he raised his eyes and looked, beyond the panes, into the distance.

— I must talk to you — he observed coldly — about the question of the Institute you run, the Institute I have the honour and the burden of being the president of, in virtue of the power delegated to me by X. I am sure you received my registered letter some time ago, telling you that I wanted to see a closer collaboration develop between our Institute and the local branch of Mistica, which has its office in the same palace as the Institute. Some days ago the Board of Directors

140

discussed the problem in your absence. . . . Your justifiable absence, I'm sure.

— It was certainly justified — Federigo remarked — because I had obtained from your Lordship five days of leave for a family funeral.

— Let us grant then that it was justified — the Count conceded — and perhaps useful as well, since it enabled us to examine your anomalous situation more closely. The thing's perfectly clear. Ten years have passed since this Commune delegated responsibility to you—and it was by no means minor responsibility—without asking, as it perhaps should have done, for any guarantees of a political nature. Perhaps the Marquis G., my predecessor, had too much faith in your discretion and thought that you yourself would have provided guarantees in accordance with changed circumstances. Now it is too late, even if you intend doing so. On the other hand—I'm sure you'll understand this—it's rather too much of a good thing that a man without elementary allegiances . . . hem, hem [the Count coughed, without specifying quite what he was going to say] should run a cultural centre that is in line with political directives. I'm not going to discuss the reasons which prevented you from providing such an undertaking . . . singular though they seem. However, I must inform you that next Thursday you must hand over authority to a successor who will be named within the next two days. I take it the accounts are in order? In any case they shouldn't take long.

— The accounts are not in order — Federigo stammered. — I have received no salary for the last eighteen months, moreover I have paid the staff from my own pocket during the last three months . . . assuming I'd be recompensed.

— Ah, — the Count said — you've never informed us about all this?

— Signor Conte, I sent you at least ten memorandums.

— Of course, of course . . . — the Count admitted. — You will have the money as soon as possible. As regards the redundancy money that you are owed, I think a letter of voluntary resignation on your part would simplify matters. You agree that you yourself want to be relieved of the job, and that you will make no unfavourable comment? The administration of the Institute, being absolved of all responsibility, might not reject the idea of granting you a small bonus, some tangible compensation. . . . I hope I have explained the situation clearly enough.

— Making a considerable saving on my redundancy money — Federigo replied surprisingly sharply.

— *Oh, peu de chose* — the Count said offhandedly — you are part of a semi-private institute that has not been recognised as such. We have taken the right steps at the right time. I am waiting for your voluntary resignation.

— And if it does not come? — Federigo inquired, increasingly surprised at his own audacity.

— In that case — the Count concluded, raising his arm as a sign of leave-taking — we shall shoot low, don't make any mistake.

Federigo in his turn also raised his arm and made a right about-turn. A few seconds later he had descended the stairs of the Commune palace and reached his now empty church-cum-library. The letter from the stranger in Seattle (Washington) remained on his desk half-answered. Federigo took up his pen, cleaned the nib, and went on to finish the letter in bad English: *As for Mr. Fruscoli's shop I beg to inform you.* . . . He finished writing, put the letter in an envelope, stamped it from his own pocket, and reflected in a melancholy way that in future no letter from Seattle would receive any answer. After that he locked the door and, head bowed, walked away in the direction of the post office.

Poetry Does Not Exist

The curfew had started and the two men, who used to sleep at my house for safety reasons, had returned some minutes ago. Of the two temporary guests, one was my friend Brunetto, a physicist and researcher in ultrasonics and an experienced conspirator. It was he who contributed an element of stability, being the permanent or semi-permanent owner of this house. But the other fellow was not so much a guest on the run as a ghost on the run, who every evening assumed a series of phantom figures whose names and identity were carefully concealed.

The dismal evening in 1944 had begun with the city still living under the incubus of endless strafing and retaliation. On that occasion it was Giovanni's turn—a grey-haired docile-looking man in desperate need of escape. It was very cold and the two visitors were sitting near the radio, their fingers stretched towards the electric stove, when the internal telephone rang from the porter's lodge.

— Look out, a German's coming up.

There was no time to lose. I made a signal and Bruno and Giovanni disappeared into their dark room. I myself having switched the radio to a local station, walked towards the door, waiting for the bell to ring. What could my friends do? And what could I do in such a situation? There were no emergency exits, and the German may not have been alone. The bell rang—softly at first, and then more loudly. I let a few seconds pass, pretending to be coming from the other end of the corridor. I unbolted the door. The German was little more than twenty years old, nearly six foot, with a hooked nose like a bird of prey, and eyes half-way between timid and frantic, under a tuft of bushy eyebrows. He took off his cap, and having checked up in his laboured Italian that I was really myself, pulled out a roll of paper, and pointed it at me.

— I'm a 'literary' — he said — I've brought the poems you

asked for. I'm from Stuttgart and my name is Ulrich K. — Ulrich K., oh yes, your name is quite familiar to me — I said, plainly flattered, and ushered the man (a sergeant) to the room where the radio was. — It's a great honour. What can I do for you?

I was completely in the dark, but after a few seconds I managed to find my bearings. He was a stranger who had written to me some two years back, about his translations of Italian poets, and to whom I had written or had got somebody to write, asking for a collected edition of Hölderlin's lyrics, which in those days were not to be found in Italian bookshops. He explained that the book was out of stock even in Germany and that he had brought me a typed copy of about three hundred pages. He apologised for having transcribed the Zinkernagel text rather than the Hellingrath one. But then I myself could easily rearrange the material in a couple of months, which was no great problem. What was I supposed to pay him? Not a *pfennig*. He was glad to have helped *sein gnadiger Kollege*. If anything, I could perhaps copy out some of our own more illustrious contemporary writers. (I was in a cold sweat and not only at the prospect of the labour involved.) He had only been in Italy a short time, working as an accountant in a small store run by the Germans. At first the Germans were afraid of local hostility, but later on things improved, so that in spite of the curfew they managed to organise concerts in the public square. Among them there were three shirkers, who were professional musicians. My visitor himself used to play. I'm not sure whether a hornpipe or a fife. And what about his profession, his career? At first, he'd been a student of philosophy. But he was not prepared to accept that philosophical speculation was a serpent that ate its own tail, a turning of thought on itself. He felt it his duty to explain the meaning of Life, but couldn't. He had fallen into the hands of a master who dismantled the systems of others in order to expose their unresolvable doubts, their inner contradictions. The only ultimate certainty was that of anguish, failure, frustration. He had asked if it was worth someone's while getting rid of the old systems of metaphysics in order to arrive at such a conclusion. The master, having got fed up with him, gently accompanied him to the door. (A glass of wine? Why not, even more than one, but after you, please, thanks, *bitte, bitte schön*). Soon after, my German friend's mind turned to poetry, but not to the poetry of the vulgar belletristic type. Here, too, things became complicated. Ancient poetry is almost inaccessible. Homer is not a man; every deviation from what is human is something extraneous. The Greek lyric poets were not all that fragmentary, as they come down to us, and we in fact lack the right perspective to judge them. And where should we find that sacred element which alone would enable us to understand the great writers of tragedies? Let us not talk of Pindar since we are so far away from his mythical, agnostic and musical world, and let us forget about the oratory and didacticism of the Latin writers. And what about Dante? A very great poet indeed, but then one reads him as one reads a *pensum*: a Ptolemaic man who lived in a box of matches (all used) and hence something quite far removed from us. And Shakespeare? He, admittedly, is very great, but too naturalistic. Goethe's was quite a different case. He was already working in the full stream of neo-classicism.

— And the moderns? — I asked him, swallowing the last drop of yellow-label Chianti.

— Oh, the moderns, my distinguished colleague — Ulrich replied with a glint in his eye — we shall create them through our collaboration. They're an unpredictable lot, and we're too much a part of them to be able to judge them objectively. Take it from me—poetry doesn't exist. With ancient poetry we can't identify ourselves. And as for modern poetry it's repugnant like everything else that's modern. It's got no history, no form, no style. And yet, and yet . . . a perfect poem should be like a philosophical system that works—the end of life, an explosion, a collapse—whereas an imperfect poem's not a poem at all. It's much better scuffling . . . with girls. But you know they're shy? Which is a great pity! (He repeated in French: *C'est dommage.*)

He got up, tilted the bottle to see if it was really empty, and bowed, wishing me good reading of his Hölderlin. I didn't have the courage to tell him that I had given up German two years ago. In the corridor he put his cap on askew, and bowed again. In a matter of seconds he was swallowed up by the lift.

I stopped outside the room in the corridor and opened it softly. My guests had remained in the dark all this time.

— Is your German friend gone? — Bruno asked — And what did he say?

— He said that poetry doesn't exist.

— Ah!

Giovanni turned his back and began to snore. They were both lying in the same narrow bed.

Part IV

The Man in Pyjamas

I was walking up and down the corridor in slippers and pyjamas, stepping from time to time over a heap of dirty linen. It was an A class hotel. It had two lifts and one goods lift which were almost always out of order, but there was no store-room for sheets, pillow-slips and towels in temporary disuse, and the chambermaids had to pile them up where they could, that is, in all sorts of odd corners. Late at night I used to visit these corners and because of this the chambermaids never liked me. However, by tipping them I had, as it were, obtained their tacit consent to stroll wherever I wanted. It was past midnight and I heard the telephone ring softly. Could it be in my room? I glided stealthily towards it, but noticed that it was ringing in a room adjacent to mine—room 22. As I was returning I overheard a woman's voice on the phone, saying: 'Don't come yet, Attilio; there's a man in pyjamas walking up and down the corridor. He might see you.'

From the other end of the line I heard an indistinct chatter. 'Oh,' she answered, 'I don't know who he is—a poor wretch who's always hanging around. Please, don't come. In any case I'll let you know.' She put the receiver down with a bang. I heard her footsteps in the room. I slipped hurriedly towards the far end of the corridor where there was a sofa, another pile of linen and a wall. But I could hear the door of room 22 open and I gathered that the woman was watching me through the slit. I could not stay where I was for long, so I slowly returned. In something like ten seconds I was to pass her room and I considered the various alternatives: (1) to return to my room and lock myself up; (2) the same, but with a difference, that is to say, to inform the lady that I had overheard everything and that I intended to do her a favour by retiring; (3) to ask her if she was really all that keen on having Attilio, or if I was merely used as pretext to avoid a rather disagreeable nocturnal bullfight; (4) to ignore the telephone

151

conversation and carry on my stroll; (5) to ask if she might eventually care to substitute me for Attilio for the object referred to in alternative number 3; (6) to demand explanation for the nomenclature 'poor wretch' with which she had chosen to designate me; (7) . . . there was some difficulty in formulating the seventh alternative. But by this time I was already in front of the slit. Two dark eyes, a crimson bed-jacket worn over a silk skirt, and short curly hair. Just a brief second and the opening shut again with a snap. My heart was beating fast as I entered my room and heard the telephone ring again next door. The woman was saying something in a soft voice which I did not catch. Like a wolf I shot back to the corridor and tried to make out what she was saying. 'It's impossible, Attilio, I say it's impossible. . . .' And then the clack of the telephone followed by the sound of her footsteps nearing the door. I made a dash towards the second pile of dirty linen, turning over in my mind alternatives 2, 3 and 5. The door opened again narrowly and it was now impossible for me to stand still. . . . I said to myself: I *am* a poor wretch, but how could *she* know that? And what if by my walking up and down the corridor I may not have perhaps saved her from Attilio? Or saved Attilio from her? I am not born to be an arbiter of anything, much less an arbiter of the life of others. I returned to my room, kicking along a pillow-slip with a slipper. This time the door opened rather wider and the curly head projected a little further. I was just about a yard away from it when, having kicked off the slipper and come to attention, I bellowed out in a voice that could be heard right down the corridor: 'I have finished walking up and down, Madam. But how do you know that I am a poor wretch?'

'We all are,' she snapped and slammed the door. The telephone was ringing again.

Fatalistic attitude

An English Gentleman

I know a gentleman who spends his Christmas holidays in Switzerland where he practises a sport invented by him—that of the 'bogus Englishman'. I know why he plays this role outside England. In the British Isles the English are a common commodity; they neither love themselves nor love the foreign visitors, and they can't decently play 'the Englishman' in their own country. One needs a different environment in order to play this role—a well-bred and neutral world, looking quite comfortable without really being so. Basically untamed, busy and hard-working, Albion is the last country in the world where one can gain anything by playing the role of an Englishman.

In all probability the bogus Englishman I know, and whom I have myself been trying for years to emulate in vain, has failed to keep his own identity secret from the management of his hotel and from its sharp-eyed *concierge*. But it does not matter. The game starts only after he has handed over his passport. It involves avoiding any sporting manifestation whatsoever, staying all day in the hall, and having tea and cakes at the proper hour, accepting the menu of the hotel without making any fuss, even if it consists of such abominable dishes as the Italian guests, after having shouted picturesque imprecations in Roman dialect, get replaced with bleeding steaks or striped *paillards* of veal.

If, for example, the menu contains Irish stew, a sweetish mixture of boiled mutton, carrots and tinned peas, the bogus Englishman will eat up every bit of goat-meat, carrot and pea, and will swallow them with religious care, as if each morning at home he were eating an endless quantity of kippers and porridge.

The bogus Englishman smokes Dutch cigars and drinks the coffee they serve him, without asking for percolated coffee. Sprawling in an armchair, he spends his afternoons reading articles on the Bernese oligarchy of the eighteenth century and on the great Gibbon's opinions concerning it; he diligently scrutinises the news in the *Gazette de Lausanne* and makes it a point not to miss the deaths, and perhaps winds up his day going cursorily through a hotel library book picked up from among the most harmless kind, ranging from Wilkie Collins to Ouida. The bogus Englishman is polite to everyone but talks to none. Only an occasional 'K'you' comes out of his mouth if other foreigners or waiters show him some courtesy. In the evening the bogus Englishman wears the black suit, which the Italians—not the English—call a *smoking*, and wears it with quite an off-hand manner as if he had been doing it for years. On New Year's Eve the bogus Englishman attends the *réveillon*, but he does not dance, either because he doesn't know how to or he just has no one to dance with.

He orders a bucket with a bottle of *champagne brut*, lets them put a coloured hat on his head, blows a horn along with the others, wrapped in streamers and looking both happy and dazed. When midnight chimes, and the orchestra stops, and the room is thrown into momentary darkness and everyone stands up and raises his glass, and corks pop, and people start drinking toasts and greeting and embracing each other, the bogus Englishman also gets up, raises the stem of his glass and drinks to his own health or to that of some far-off person. And if the dancing starts again he rises in a dignified manner, murmurs a 'K'you' of thanks to those who give way for him, and to the attendant who opens the door for him, and then retires in a dignified manner to his room.

The next day he is one of the first down for breakfast, in his grey suit. He has the air of being resigned to the little 'Continental' meal without porridge and without Palethorp's sausages, and is satisfied with tea and slices of buttered bread. The hotel is empty; others are either still lying asleep or have made for the funiculars with their winter outfits which make them look like bears. The bogus Englishman reclines in an armchair, and removes the bookmark from an old unreadable novel. He is watching the snowflakes fluttering about the window-panes, and trying to light the cigar first with a lighter which naturally doesn't work, and then with a match-box, from which there arises a very pleasant curl of smoke. He then bends his head, reads something, swims in the smoke, sleeps, dreams. Tomorrow he leaves. For where? I alone know his destination.

I don't know his name, but I sometimes come across him in the streets of Milan where he seems to be completely transformed into a talkative and bored inhabitant of the Lombard capital. I don't know if he has also noticed me as I have noticed him. Nor do I know if he realises that for years I have been assiduously trying to imitate him, but in vain, or if he has ever been to England and felt the same admiration and boredom that I felt. All I know is that in a hypothetical Association of Bogus Englishmen he ought to be made President and I Vice-President.

Sul Limite

The early part of the journey I am going to describe was preceded by a nasty incident. I had left my friends' house in Via delle Carra, and after walking a few steps had found a taxi which I hoped would take me to Piazza Beccaria. As the taxi was going through the Prato I saw a green Chevrolet heading towards us from a tram-crossing. There was plenty of time to stop had either driver had any sense. But neither was prepared to do so, each insisting obstinately on his right to 'precedenza'. The distance between the two cars became shorter and shorter. 'Another stupid accident,' I said to myself as I shut my eyes. After an infinitesimal fraction of time, which seemed like an eternity, there was the most violent crash, and I was tossed, like a dice, around the dark cabin of the taxi. It had evidently turned over and I found myself lying flat on the roof. Light filtered in through a broken pane and I could hear the voices of the people gathered outside. The two drivers were having a heated argument, with the crowd dividing into two groups and taking sides. No one seemed to worry about me. 'But there's a man inside,' said a kind-hearted person at last. Someone tried to open the door which I was leaning against, with the result that I immediately rolled out on to the street and picked myself up. At this point the exchange of oaths between the drivers had reached a climax, so it seemed a suitable moment for me to brush down my coat as best I could, pinch myself to ensure that I was still alive and jump into a passing tram. The tram was half-empty; everybody had got off at the Porta and even the conductor had got out to have a smoke. However, the tram set off again pretty soon without the conductor, and within a few minutes I realised that I had reached the outskirts of the town, exactly opposite to where I wanted to go.

The tram stopped inside a wooden hangar and the driver told me that this was the terminus and asked me to get off. A few seconds later, the tram left again, leaving me alone. It was spring, but already quite warm. To judge from the light it must have been about six o'clock in the afternoon, although I should have thought it was later.

As I was feeling for my watch, I saw, coming along a path, a trap pulled by a Sardinian donkey and driven by a young man wearing pyjamas. On his head was a featherless Tyrolean hat. Sitting snugly beside the young man was a tiny reddish dog of doubtful breed, which kept barking at me.

A pull on the brake, a tightening of the reins and the trap came to a halt. The dog, wildly excited and panting, jumped playfully up at me, tottering on its hind legs. The pyjama-clad youth came towards me smiling politely and said:

— Don't you recognise me? I'm not surprised though, after such a long time. I am Nicola.

— Nicola? — I said . . . — Nicola . . . who?

— Nicola is my surname, my dear friend—the N.C.O. in the Alpinists, who left the marching battalion at Negrar with you, and came up on the Loner and the Corno as a volunteer. Don't you remember? I know; after all we only knew each other for a couple of days. You were the last person I met then. Perhaps that's why I remember you so vividly. Shortly after, I was hit by shrapnel and came here. All kinds of scrap-iron pelted down at us on the bed of the Leno. Don't you remember? But you were in a different battalion and perhaps never got to know about this . . .

— Nicola . . . of course. . . . I remember perfectly well — I said, turning pale with fright. — How very nice. Exploding shrapnel . . . of course . . . read about it in divisional news. Nicola—what a surprise to see you again!

— And I am not alone here, you see. Galiffa's with me too—the little dog you used to like as a child, and Ponochietto, Vittoria Apuana's little donkey you used to give sugar to. Aren't I in good company? — and he gave a laugh which made me shiver.

— Galliffa . . . Pinochietto . . . — I stammered. — But, tell me,

157

how do you know all this? Didn't you . . . come over here . . . on your own?

The donkey and the dog kept licking my hands, showing obvious signs of recognition. I didn't have any sugar with me and felt quite put out by this unexpected encounter. Nicola laughed in a superior way and beckoned to me to climb up beside him.

— I work in the clearing office, at Limite — he said — and when I heard your name I went through the whole film of your life. I had been through it before, and so knew to the very minute when I could expect you. But what can one do? There's a lot of work to be done here and not enough people to do it. So you've rather taken me by surprise. Otherwise I'd have been here to meet you with all the animals from your private ark. Fufi, Gastoncino, Passepoil, Bubú, Buck, Valentina. . . . But don't worry, you'll be able to see them all again.

— Ah, even Valentina, I wondered. (It must have been the tortoise which used to come into the kitchen to snuggle up to Buck, the wolf. . . . How many years ago?)

— Actually it would have been better if I'd brought Mimì with me in the bottle, in which the conjuror used to keep her; but it was getting late and I wanted to be here to meet you when you arrived. But you'll also see Mimì soon. Giovanna's looking after her.

— Mimì in a bottle . . . of course. . . . (Was it the guinea-pig I'd had a century ago? But then who was Giovanna? An animal or a person? I felt my heart sink. Giovanna! Could it possibly be . . . her?)

— Giovanna — Nicola confirmed driving the donkey towards some lush-looking plantations. — She's at Limite too, and she even manages to look after the Zoo.

— Is she dead? — I asked without raising my eyes and swaying on the narrow seat. I started smoking a butt; it seemed strangely tasteless. — And . . . is she all right?

— She's alive — he retorted sharply; — though you can call her dead if you like, the same as you and me.

— Ah — I stuttered. And the feeling of certainty made me bow my head. Then I opened my eyes again. The trap was passing some sheds where women were standing in queues waiting for something. All around the country looked colourless and in the distance one could see a group of white houses.

— You're a bit shocked, aren't you? — grunted Nicola with an attempt at gaiety — I know. At first one still feels tied to the past. The same thing used to happen to me when I was among the living—oh what am I saying?—I mean among the dead of the Antelimite where I've just come from to meet you. I used to dream and on waking up, I would still remember the dream. But after a time the memory of that dream would fade. That's what's happening to you now. There's still an earthly residue left in you which has to settle down in your mind; it will only take a short time. Later on, when Giovanna shows you the 'recording' of what you call your life, you'll find it hard to recognise. It is like that up to Zone I, the station where Jack and Fred often go. Fred's the man who drew your portrait at Spoleto, don't you remember? This memory too will gradually fade away and a new one will take its place. To tell the truth Giovanna and I should have reached the new destination by now. I think they have recognised our abilities at the Centre. But then, you see, we are of more use at Limite, for Giovanna is an extremely accomplished interpreter. She has always had a flair for languages, and I can assure you she is in great demand here. I'm sure there'd be a lot of work for her to do in Zone II as well as at the Institute where the process of de-materialisation starts. From what we've heard of the place, it doesn't seem to be very promising. It seems to have a very strict rationing system and it is short of accommodation. Your father promised to let us know what it's like there, but so far. . . . That's why we've decided to stay on at Limite.

As he talked, Nicola kept whipping the donkey, and the town perched neatly on top of a hill, accessible only by a flight of steps, drew nearer and nearer. The trees in the valley were stunted and monotonous and the sun appeared to be stationary on the horizon. I threw away the cigarette-end.

— Shall I — I said, sweating with terror, — shall I have to stay with you too?

—Yes, of course, for the time being at any rate. However, it'll depend on Fred. Poor Fred, do you know he was very jealous of you? He's not a bad fellow, but he's not much use here. As to his other life, I expect you know how it happened, in a quarrel with some drunks. But how he missed Giovanna! When we saw her and Jack in the film sealed up with lead, he raved like a madman. He wanted to be the only one to go and meet them. It was through you that I got to know them and we became friends. They'll be sorry not to have been able to come and meet you. But what can one do? These are the privileges of the man working at the arrival office, who's in a position to look through thousands of individual films. If you like, we could go through a bit of yours this evening. We'll choose some harmless scene, of course, which wouldn't make Fred . . . unhappy. As far as I'm concerned I can look at anything. Although the oldest here, I'm the youngest of you all. And after all, Jack's such a good fellow . . . so accommodating.

I was hunched up on the seat. Galiffa kept licking my hands affectionately and the donkey twitched his ears as the whip hit him. And then: — Nicola — I managed to say. The trap turned sharply down an avenue of what looked like horse-chestnuts, at the far end of which a row of sparkling white houses blocked the view.

— Yes? — Nicola inquired, cracking the whip light-heartedly in the air.

— Can't this business be postponed? I mean, this meeting? Can't you see that so far as I'm concerned, it's all over. I've worked so hard all these years to be able to keep my mind off these . . . friends; I thought the effort would drive me mad. And now you. . . . No, no, it's too much, too much. . . . You see, I wanted something that had a beginning and an end in my own lifetime. Something that was eternal precisely because it was finite. I can't start this all over again. No Nicola, I can't; take me to my mother . . . if she's there.

— You'll be able to communicate with Zone III later on. The last time I heard from her she was well. But in that Zone, I must warn you, memory deteriorates fast. Stay with us for a few decades; you'll get used to it. Look at me. Can't you see how young I've stayed?

Pinochietto stopped in front of a building. From an open window on the ground floor I could hear the ticking of one of those portable alarm-clocks called *Noiseless*. Nicola jumped down and held out his hand to me. Galiffa was lying comfortably asleep in my arms.

— She's the one who's working overtime — he whispered to me. — Come, have courage, she hasn't changed. I know you wanted to forget. But start living with us . . . friends who got here before you.

going back again

On the Beach

The yellow card that I found this morning on the sand where I usually lie in the sun beside the newspapers and the deck-chair, a few steps from the Pensione Hunger's beach umbrellas, informed me that there was a parcel for me from the U.S.A. If it was not collected by the 28th of the month, it would go to the Red Cross. A parcel from whom! And addressed to me? As if to satisfy my legitimate curiosity I also received a post-card from abroad which had been redirected from Florence. It explained everything. It was from a Miss Bronzetti who remembered me and who thought she would send me some cocoa and other titbits. She hoped that I was well, sent me her warmest regards, and remembered how very patient I had been with her cat which used to steal meat from the butcher's shop on the ground-floor of the house where I lived. More greetings followed, a promise of more parcels, and the signature A.B. 'A.B.', I turned over in my mind. But, of course, why not? I am sure she was called Annalena or Annagilda or Annalia.

I turned to Antonio who was sitting in his deck-chair, shuffling the sand with his bare feet. He had met nearly all my acquaintances of the last few years, so perhaps he would remember something more about this person.

— Anactoria or Annabella — he confirmed. — I remember her very well. She used to live somewhere near San Gervasio. She was from Vercelli or thereabouts. She had been a teacher in a college in Wisconsin or Vermont, but at that time she was on sabbatical leave and was spending the winter in Florence.

I had a flash of intuition. I recalled a popular quarter of the Cure, a spinster's neat, orderly apartment full of cheap reproductions and oleographs—Botticelli's Venus, the Masaccio al Carmine fresco, the Gozzoli angels—and books of all sorts, paperbacks, books from lending libraries, books with inhuman and, for me, pretty intimidating titles: *Misunderstood*, *Kidnapped*,

Upstarts . . . even a pocket edition of Dante in English, together with the original, and a collection of thirteenth-century hymns. And in the midst of all this Annabella or Anactoria, the tiny, slim tenacious Piedmontese whom twenty or thirty years of teaching in the United States—training generations of girls in the rudiments of our language—had endeared to Italy, the country which had continued to be hers in every epoch, every situation and every whim of the historical or political barometer. — Anactoria . . . of course, yes, I remember her perfectly — I tell Antonio, trying to impress upon him the fact that I know what I am talking about — How kind of her! I shall write to her at once—even before collecting the present from the post office. Nevertheless, it's quite a nuisance, coming to this place. . . . I must get someone else to collect it, or send my identity-card or something. . . .

To tell the truth I felt depressed as I thought about the tricks that memory plays—a sort of St. Patrick's well of remembrance. I had always thought that an infinite number of things relating to others, who were dead and forgotten, still lived on in my mind and found in me their last *raison d'être*. I thought I was rich, but now it turned out that I was poor. Someone I had completely forgotten had taken me by surprise. It was I who lived on in the mind of Anactoria or Annalena; it was I who survived in her, not she in me. But how on earth can memory fade away so completely? I was always aware of a host of possible spirits living in the casket of my memory—spirits I almost never evoked for fear of reviving shades that were not always pleasant, but that nevertheless sometimes rose to the surface of my consciousness and enriched it. Reminiscences so formed, castanets snapping unduly late, can be easily accounted for. But what about the creature that springs up like a jack-in-the-box from apparently inert material, a complete oblivion which suddenly reveals itself as a presence? In fact, I've always believed in a relative forgetfulness which is almost voluntary, a sort of Taylorian process by which the mind rejects what is no longer any use, while at the same time retaining the end of the thread. But in this instance there was no doubt at all: Anactoria or Annabella who had been buried in my mind for four, five or six years had now come back because she *wanted* to come back. It was she who had chosen to grace me with her presence, not I who had condescended to reawaken her while searching through the past in a desultory way. It was she—the amiable creature, the worthy intruder, who while digging her past up again, had come across my shade and had tried to re-establish a 'correspondence' in the best sense of the term.

— But it's the cat business that doesn't convince me — I said to Antonio. — First of all there never was a butcher's shop on the ground floor of the house I lived in. And then I would certainly have given the cat a name, and I never forget animals' names.

— But there was a cat — Antonio pointed out — a female cat which always wanted to be picked up by the neck, stroked and patted. And if you didn't do as it wished, it would mew in a rather morbid way. It must have fallen from a window or run away after a few days. The cat's mistress, I suppose, had left earlier, along with those other girls . . . Patricia . . . and whatever their names were.

— Oh Patricia, I've often thought about her. But then how on earth does Annalena fit in . . .?

The light blazed on the Apuanians in the interval between one late August storm and the next. There were relatively few people sun-bathing on the damp sand. I couldn't manage to get as tanned as I would have liked, but from behind my dark glasses I followed the movements of the last hawkers as they passed by the empty bathing-huts. Their cries reached me, unenthusiastic and monotonous: 'Blackberries, raspberries, iced drinks' . . . Then I saw the poodle leading the blind man— a dark figure *alla Velasquez*—from the folds of whose viscerally groaning harmonica *Bésame mucho* ground doggedly out. It must have been rather late.

— Of course, yes, I remember her well, I do have a good

164

memory after all. Even though officially on leave, Anastasia—I mean Anactoria—had taken on the responsibility of chaperoning the girls from Miss Clay's College, when they went out during the winter holiday from the Villa del Giramontino. Six or seven young heiresses who had gone there to acquire a bit of culture. They were studying history of art, music and dancing, as well as Fascism and other esoteric subjects. In the spring there was going to be some sort of prize-giving ceremony at the villa and the prefect—His Excellency—and three or four leaders of the local political gang were going to be there. The girls were very eager to meet them, and Miss Clay was crazy about it all. Who knows but some of them might even belong to the Italian nobility while one of them had an American wife! It must have been at one of those parties that I first met Mr. Stapps. Patricia, the most beady-eyed of them all, used to say that she had a passion for him. When she left Villa Giramontino to stay with some of the noble families in town, Anactoria was told to keep a particularly close watch on her. She would accompany her to museums, concerts, theatres, the Boboli, and when they didn't go out, she saw to it that Patricia went to bed early. But at midnight Patricia was already out with Mr. Stapps. Poor Anactoria, if only she'd known. . . . Or perhaps she did know, but didn't take Patricia to task. It was her lot to let others play with fire; but as for herself, well. . . . In any case, she was too old to dance *giava*. She had lived thirty or forty years by herself in a two-room flat in the middle of an enormous wasps' nest—a girls' college—and she would usually eat in the refectory with a group of her own students. Sometimes she would eat alone in her room. A couple of eggs fried on the electric stove in her kitchen. Every six or seven years she would come to Italy, but by now she had begun to feel rather detached and assumed on occasion an American manner. 'Back home such things don't happen,' she would say, but then when she was back there, with only student performances and second-rate concerts for distraction, she would die of nostalgia for Italy.

— Oh yes, I know, I know. We haven't been very courteous to her, Antonio. We should have written to her first, or rather while she was here, we should have taken more care of her. . . .
— Are you mad? — Antonio asked lifting his eyes from his newspaper. — Are you still thinking of that wretched girl? Send her a greetings card and have done with it. Who remembers her anyhow? We don't even know her name.

— I don't remember her name, Antonio — I said rather angrily — but I can tell you I remember everything else—only too well. The only thing that doesn't fit in is the story of the cat. Apart from that, I see it all perfectly, even what Anactoria-Anastasia has never told me, either before or now. Imagine the kind of tales about Italy that must have reached her, a thousand miles away, after the first world-war, when we had let ourselves in for being governed by a gang of thieves. Anactoria I remember didn't care a fig for His Excellency. Immune to propaganda and the baser brand of patriotism, she was—unlike many of her compatriots—justice and purity incarnate. We've realised this too late, Antonio. She used to think with her head: like me . . . and better than you.

Antonio stood up, yawned and stretched himself. A few heavy drops of rain fell on the sand and the wind began to get up, rustling the pale carpet of pine-cones. Those few left on the beach hurried towards the terrace of the Pensione Hunger where the waitresses could be seen busying themselves among the tables. The bathing attendant closed up and uprooted the remaining umbrellas. I had not heard the gong but it must have been past one.

— There's still time — Antonio observed ironically. — You can still make amends to your Anastasia. But let's go and see if the hotel cooking lives up to its reputation.

The Paintings in the Cellar

The north-east wind was blowing when B and I came out of the Revoltella Museum and proceeded in the direction of Café Garibaldi. We encountered a tall, slim youth in a gaberdine rain-coat turned half inside out by the wind. As he hurriedly passed us by, he turned round and greeted us with his hand. He was quite a commonplace boy, and yet I asked B, 'Who is he?'

'Oh, nobody in particular,' replied B nonchalantly, 'just a futurist.'

Two or three years later, still at Trieste, I went to see an exhibition of Giorgio Carmelich, who had recently died of consumption in a German sanatorium. The catalogue gave some information about the artist, who had died at the age of twenty, and on the few works of art he had left behind. There was his *opera omnia*, in front of me—about thirty items in all, pastels, gouaches and drawings, but chiefly pastels. His art did not strike me as being particularly interesting, nor was I particularly keen—at least as regards painting—on discovering new talent. However, I asked my Triestine guide's opinion of them. I was surprised by his answer.

'Don't you remember that boy,' B told me, 'that futurist we met two years ago in the square? It was he, Carmelich.'

I say that the answer surprised me because I remembered that encounter perfectly well and I wondered how both of us should remember it so vividly. I gave a close look at what was displayed, which was something half-way between the secession of Monaco and the recent central European expressionism as to style, and quite literary as to themes and subject-matter. They were characterised by a realistic obsession of a macabre kind, the *smell of horse flesh* which is typical of Kafka, Ungar and other narrative writers of Prague who were in those days very much in vogue at Trieste: skulls, deformed figures, still life in the abstract, and, of course, metaphysical landscapes;

everything mixed up in small pastels with sharp tones and chalky surface. But the painter was dead. The story of his life had come to an end. Taken all in all, from the very first to the last manifestation of what was personal in his art, there emanated something sincere and pathetic which transcended the problem, at times quite insignificant, of art and not art; he was dead. And yet I had once met Carmelich the futurist when alive; he passed by us in the north-east wind waving his hand, and I had asked about him and I hadn't forgotten him, who knows why? . . . How could I rid myself of that dead boy? Hence half an hour later when I left the exhibition, I had two pastels under my arm, bought for quite a paltry sum, even in those days. My career as an art customer started and ended there. And yet I was sure I had chosen the best that the exhibition had to offer.

The two pastels migrated with me to a city where art had, and has, altogether different roots and a more humane face. And they at once came into conflict with the house and the atmosphere in which they would live. But later on a sort of *modus vivendi* was established between me and the paintings, and we accepted the principle of mutual tolerance. The bigger and more showy pastel—the one representing Prague buried under snow, with some men in top-hats and swallow-tailed coats, pencilled beside the massive monument to John Huss and the sharp toffee and confetti-coloured houses with pointed roofs— was put in a make-shift room where the elements of the radiator were locked up for the sake of economy, and where only Agatha the seamstress and a busybody, set foot. The smaller pastel, on the other hand, a gondola in front of a grand Venetian Palace, all lace-work and mullioned windows, and on one side the shadow of the dissolving view of an equestrian monument, was accommodated, boldly enough, in the room underground where I slept, but which I never entered in the day time. It was hung to a book-shelf and there was no other painting to compete with it. The real paintings, the De Pisis, and later on a Morandi, were on the floor above which was accessible to visitors. The Carmelich was out of bounds, even though the English had not yet entered the city, or were there only as guests.

The years passed quietly for the two Carmelichs. And then one day I had to go through a very complicated process of moving out and I went from the ground floor to the fifth floor of a house which here in Tuscany would be regarded as a skyscraper. I had many books, some other paintings as well, besides trunks, chests and suitcases; and there was even less space in the new house. When everything was put in order, I realised that the two Carmelichs were missing. They were removed, I was informed by the inevitable Agatha, to the cellar with much else that was useless. I felt some remorse, but soon a new factor came into being which somehow mitigated that feeling—the war, the second world war of my life, soon forced me to consign to the cellar furniture, paintings and books that were far more important to me than the two pastels acquired so many years ago. I tried—and in fact succeeded—in saving something from the bombs which the swarms of buzzing drones let fall on the suburban parts of the city. The station of Campo di Marte was quite close, and just a few inches mistake on the part of the bombardiers was enough to. . . . But better not think of it. In the half-empty apartment only the most necessary furniture was kept as well as piles of discarded books, almost all presentation copies and verses. But the most important objects together with the De Pisis and the small Morandi were lying underground, packed up as best they could be. Still, who cared for them? There were other anxieties and hopes to occupy one's mind.

The problem has arisen only now, much later. I have descended to the cellar and have helped Agatha carry furniture, bookshelves, and papers to the upper floor. I also opened the chests, made piles of dusty books tumble on the ground, and in the process a mouse-trap went off in the dark and imprisoned my fingers. Gradually the empty apartment became full again and the books, the best paintings, and the prints of

Manzù have come to light. But the little Prague and the minia-
ture Venice of Carmelich are lying at the bottom of a trunk,
together with the cracked glasses and the *passe-partout*.

'And now what's to be done with these?' asks the impa-
tient Agatha, as she rubs her fingers. What can one do with
them, old Agatha? I wish I knew the answer. Blessed be-
the day when I gave away the big painting of Bolaffio to
a worthy collector of that painter, who offered it a decent
and lasting shelter; even though because of this gesture of
'blind indifference' I merited the arrow, a wrathful verse, of
an illustrious poet of Trieste, who was justly indignant about
it. But what can one do with the little Carmelichs, Agatha?
Can I, perhaps the last custodian of that worthy boy's secret and
his unhappiness, let them perish like that? I lean against the
door of the pantry and remain immobile in a draught. The
gondola and the monument to the great reformer shine at the
bottom of the trunk. More than twenty years have passed and
it seems to be a day. A tall lean youth crosses the square
lashed by the wind, the tails of his light overcoat are flopping
around him, he waves with his hand, and I ask absent-
mindedly: 'Who is he, Bobi?'

'Oh, nobody in particular, just a futurist,' and we walk off
towards the café.

Chage

Anguish

I am highly sensitive to the *Stimmung* of the Nordic cities and the sight of Zurich with snow covering its Gothic pinnacles and big silent cars gliding along, changing colour with the different neon signs—a spectral city, empty and at the same time teeming with life (up to five o'clock, anyway)—captivated me so much that I stood long at the double-glazed window of my room. It was about four o'clock—still another hour of life to go. My breath faintly frosted the inside pane. The room was overheated, but outside the thermometer showed twenty degrees below zero. The telephone rang. It was the hotel porter.

— There's a Frau Brentano Löwy who says she has an appointment with you. Can she come up?

— Yes, let her come up.

She must have been one of those turbaned intellectuals who had congratulated me after my lecture on the previous evening. She had asked for a tête-à-tête with me, a sort of interview for a popular illustrated magazine. She specialised in talking to great men *en pantoufles*. And in the absence of very great men, she would make do with men of middle stature, so long as they were interesting. An indiscreet bit of gossip, some background colour, a photograph and the piece was done. A professional interviewer, endowed with flair and taste, she was very highly paid, from what I could gather. She wore a green turban with a red feather, a closely fitting suit and an expensive fur coat which she immediately took off. She had dark, perhaps tinted hair and was of an indeterminate age.

— Would you like a cup of tea? — I asked.

She accepted. I rang for two cups of tea.

— I don't have many questions to ask, Mr. Montana — she said. — But here are a few. Are you in favour of a union of European States? Federal union with a partial renunciation of individual sovereignties or simply a defensive pact, an alliance based on a common army? Do you think that the peripheral action of UNESCO is useful? Are you for or against the execution of the Negro MacGee who is said to have raped an American woman? Whom would you suggest for the Nobel Peace prize? Do you think a woman's rights in Italian society are protected well enough? Do you prefer atheist existentialism or Christian? Do you think that figurative art still has any meaning? Are you for or against euthanasia? Do you think that a basic European language is an urgent necessity? In the case of such a language do you think that a three per cent Italian ingredient would be enough?

She stopped, sipped her tea, and then went on:

— Quite simple things, you see. Let me add a few personal questions. Are you fond of animals? Which ones do you like best? Do you prefer cats to dogs or *vice versa*? Have you done your bit towards fighting vivisection?

She stopped and looked at me through her glasses. There was a moment's silence broken by the chimes of a pendulum.

— I always thought I preferred cats to dogs — I said, apologising for starting with the simpler questions. — But then the hysterical passion of some women for the cat tribe around them made my taste turn towards dogs. But my conversion is a recent one and it's because dogs stay in the memory longer than cats, and thus ensure for themselves a kind of survival in us. Theoretically I am against survival and I believe that it would be more dignified if man and animal could accept an endless slumber in the eternal Nothing. But of course—by heredity—I am a Christian and I can't help thinking that something of ourselves may and perhaps will last. My dog Galiffa—I can show you his photograph—died more than forty years ago. In this, the only existing photo, you can see him with a friend of mine, who is also dead. I am therefore the only person who still remembers that gay mongrel with the reddish coat. He loved me, and I too began to love him but only when it was too late.

— Passepoil — I continued — was my second dog, a Scottish terrier of very doubtful breed. We never really took to each other, so I gave him away to friends. I don't have a picture of him, but perhaps in the canine Elysian Fields, it still remembers how I once saved it from being run over. My third dog was Buck, an Alsatian. It was a very nice dog, and it adored my tortoise whose food it shared. When it got distemper, I sent it away to be looked after by peasants in Val di Pesa near Florence. But the night after it got there it ran away and came home—a distance of some twenty miles. Its distemper got worse and it had to be put down. I couldn't bear to see it dead. Euthanasia or almost. You see, Frau Brentano, we have already touched on the subject. Pippo, my fourth dog was a Schnautzer. It was born in Olga Löser's villa, a house situated among olive trees and containing eight paintings by Cézanne. Its old owner is dead, and I'm still alive. Pippo is alive too and lives in a town in the Marche. He was very touchy and never forgave me for giving him away as a present. But then I reached a certain point in my life when it became impossible to keep a dog.
— Oh, life! — Said Frau B. L. with a deep sigh — life in Italy! I have the most wonderful memories of Italy, I've spent a lot of time there. A fabulous country, but the men . . . if only you knew how I had to struggle. . . . Always lying in wait! Are you like the others too? Or are you different?

A tear furrowed her cheek, trickling with some difficulty over her powder, and her two beady eyes scrutinised me.

Half-choking I murmured:
— Yes, Frau B. L. I'm different, very different (and sensing a certain disappointment on her part) . . . but, at bottom, no, not all that different (and fearing an aggressive gesture) . . . yet, after all, I think yes, different, different from everybody else. — I was sweating, for somehow every word seemed wrong.

The telephone rang. — Frau Brentano's car has arrived — the porter announced.
— Thank you for your interesting observations, Mr. Fontale —

she got out her lip-stick. — I shall draw attention to them. With a nod she went out. She subsequently sent me a cutting of the interview. There was no mention of the dogs or ambushes, but of Herr Puntale and the modern problem of Anguish.

The New Year's Eve
Dinner

— Did you book a table, Sir? — the *maître* asked as he went through his list. — Your name, please. Pantaleoni? That's O.K. sir. We have reserved table 15 for you. It's right in the centre and away from the orchestra, as you asked.

— The menu, please.

— Here you are, Sir. Crema Parmentier, sole *alla mugnaia*, guinea-fowl on the spit, red chicory from Trieste. Peach Melba and sparkling wine: Italian, of course, not foreign.

— Only 4,500 lira for that — the customer made a wry face. I can't say I feel like complimenting you on your imagination. I'd like something better.

— Would you like to eat *à la carte*, Sir? I should have a look at the menu. There's a wide choice.

With his brows knit, Mr. Pantaleoni bent over what looked like a highly ornate papyrus. Then irritably thumping the table with his fist, he said:

— I'd like a word with the chef and the wine-waiter. There are too many things here. I want to know what sort of death I'm going to die.

The *maître* shrugged his shoulders and went away. He returned shortly with the chef and the wine-waiter—the latter with a formidable-looking leather-bound volume.

— Well, friends, I wanted to have a word with you — Mr. Pantaleoni began. — I don't mind the expense, but I want to eat like a king. And I don't know where to start. Of course, I could begin with caviare on toast and vodka, but if you don't mind I think I'd like to have Tuscan beans with a flask of wine. Is that all right, chef? Just a small quantity of warm beans, and a bowl of broth with a few drops of sherry. The sherry must be dry and slightly bitter, Tocòn for example. Do you have Tocòn? Oh, you're an angel. Now let's look at the main courses. I must admit I am tempted by a slice of grilled Adriatic turbot. But is it really from the Adriatic or does it come from Basle like your atrocious soles? If you feel like recommending it to me, I shall certainly try it. Just as it is, with lemon and parsley, or with tartar sauce, whichever you think best. But now I'm not sure whether to have something roasted or stewed—roast woodcock or stewed boar. Uhm. Do you think you could give me stewed lamb's liver and potatoes? It's a dish that should be cooked rather slowly. And please don't forget to put just a touch of catmint in it. Yes, make a note of it, *maître*. Then there's the question of dessert. Personally, I could do without, but I suppose one ought to observe the rules. Let's try the *crêpes al Grand Marnier*. I bet almost nobody knows how to make it properly; well we'll see. Thanks chef, that'll be all. And now the wines. A white Valtellina goes well with the fish, doesn't it, waiter? I'm not sure, though, whether a light red wine is the thing to have with the liver. A *rosé d'Anjou*? Let's try that. And with the dessert I might have a good bottle of Rhoederer or Charles Heidsieck, but it must be vintage. I can count on you, can't I? And now that we're alone, *maître*, can we settle the bill?

— Oh, there's no hurry, Sir. It can be done later on.

— No, I should like to pay the bill right now.

The *maître* looked slightly puzzled. Then he went to consult with the wine-waiter, made a note and came back with the bill.

— 23,500 lira — Mr. Pantaleoni observed — including taxes and service. Fine. Here are twenty-five thousand, you can keep the rest. As regards . . .

— Yes, Sir.

— Please tell the cook not to bother about cooking any of this feast for me; unless you and your staff want to dispose of it, and drink to my health. On my table I won't have anything except a plate of nut shells, a cup of camomile and an empty sparkling wine bottle. Obviously, in front of the other customers, I must look as if I've already eaten. To tell the truth, as you might have gathered, it's not my food that interests me, but other people's. Is that clear?

— ?

— I used to be a heavy eater until I became a *gourmet*. But now my only pleasure in life is seeing others eat. Those who know about this weakness of mine call me the Seer. In fact I'm not an inquisitive person: I'm simply an Epicurean moralist. Not being able to study Man in all his aspects and capacities, I've chosen his most regular and pleasant habit of eating. From the way people eat, from the choice of what they eat, and from the way they behave during their meals, I can reach some general conclusions about causes and effects. Is that clear?

— ?

— I understand your perplexity. Why don't I invite people home for dinner and watch their reactions? Firstly, it would be much more expensive. And then a guest isn't free to choose, so both his movements and his reactions are conditioned. To these two considerations add the fact that the sort of people I could invite would all belong to the same type—and not always the most interesting type. Of course, I could work as a waiter in a restaurant or as a street musician strumming my guitar in public houses, but then I wouldn't be able to observe people with such intensity. The only way of doing this is the one I have chosen for myself: that is to say, sit at a table and order at least a dozen expensive dishes one after the other. If the gutting or squeezing of some rare bird, or the blaze coming out of the stove, should have any undue effect on my salivary glands, I can follow the operation at close quarters, pretending to take a telephone call. By the way, my dear *maître*, let me make a special request with regard to this: every time I make a sign, please ask the waiter to come and tell me that a long-distance telephone call has come through so that I can get up, pass by the most interesting table, and follow the operation in every detail. Of course, I shall make a point of walking to and fro as slowly as possible. I identify myself with everything to the point of getting indigestion or getting drunk. That's why my doctor has warned me not to overdo it. At a certain age even the Seer must take care of his health. But look, here are the first customers. Now, dear *maître*, please make sure that nobody suspects anything. Get my table properly prepared and call me whenever there's something worth watching at close quarters. Watch for my signs like a hawk. You know, I'm in your hands, *cher maître*.

— Rest assured, Sir. We'll see to everything just as you want.

In about two inches of water in one of those zinc baths used for keeping salt cod soft, a lobster was sticking out—a common species, of the kind immortalised in Lewis Carroll's *Alice*. Its shell was a colour mid-way between the blue of a shark and a mouldy green; its eyes were like black buttons shining on the ends of dry twigs; and its thick claws were tightly bound together with string. If anyone raised his finger to touch it, the lobster, keenly following the movement of the finger, would suddenly lift one of its claws, as if it was going to rip off the finger-tip. But the string prevented it from doing so, and its lethal shears fell back into the water.

We were in Trieste and had stopped at a fish-shop on the promenade. The sky was overcast and it had started to drizzle.
— In half an hour or so, it'll be in the saucepan — said a man in glasses — and yet it's still trying to attack. The aggressive instinct never entirely dies either in men or in beasts, it seems.
— I think it's more a question of the defensive instinct — observed a man in a beret. — It only claws those who try to catch it and eat it. It's not its fault after all.
— But — said a third man — who knows how many oysters it's cut open with those garden shears? Oysters and clams and mussels. Lobsters are very greedy about mussels.

Each of the three raised his finger in turn and each time the lobster raised and then dropped his claw. Its little eyes were very alert and unapprehensive.
— I think it's playing like a cat — the second man commented.
— It doesn't mean any harm. A cat scratches in fun too. Perhaps it doesn't realise it's doomed, though it must know its claws are of no avail.
— It knows perfectly well what's going to happen to it — said the first man — and it's trying to sell its skin, or rather its shell, at a good price. When it's boiled, it'll go purple, a sort

of cardinal red. The claws are the best part; soft and rather jelly-like; the rest . . .

This made them all start licking their lips and as they moved on another group of spectators rolled up.

— It's the classical *homard* which the French prefer to crayfish — a tall thin young man remarked to an older one. It's very expensive in France. In Paris you'll find *homard à l'americaine* on every menu.

— That's a spelling mistake! *Originally it was homard à l'armoricaine* — said the old man. — When I was *sous-chef* at the Ritz that's how they used to write it. How times have changed!

— Oh, what a nice crayfish! — said a child. — Can I touch it, papa? — And before his father could say 'yes' or 'no', the child had put his tiny finger into the tub, untying the string in the process. The lobster closed its claws, pausing a few seconds round the finger as if to stroke it; then it let go. Everybody shouted: 'Watch out! let it go!' but the finger hadn't the slightest scratch on it. In the meantime the fishmonger had seen what had happened and lifted the lobster up in his hand to tie the string round it again. But with a flip of its tail, the lobster shot to the ground and hobbling on its claws and tail, headed for the quay as if to plunge back into the water. There was a brief chase, and a slight scuffle around the fugitive. In a few seconds it had been bundled up, still struggling, in a piece of yellow paper, and put on the scales. Who wanted it? It was offered at a reduced price to get rid of it. All eyes were fixed on the customer who took away the strange shapeless package from which came a weary click-click of claws.

— Are they going to boil it? — the child protested. — But why? It was only playing with me.

— Yes, it's going to be boiled alive — came the answer.

— In a saucepan! — remarked the old *sous-chef*. — I used to put them in the oven with a good drop of brandy before they got cold. But who'd think of doing that now?

He put up his umbrella and walked off, still talking about old menus at the Ritz.

The Flight of the Hawk

It is raining cats and dogs. Behind the inner courtyard and beyond the tortuous zig-zag of the roofs stands the tangled skeleton of a tall, bare tree. The fitful showers of rain alternately make it disappear and re-emerge and give it the appearance of a sharply incised engraving or a faded pastel. Now a black dot descends from the sky and settles on the loftiest branch, a thin twisted bough that immediately bends under the weight. Judging from the way the bough bends and from the black mark the bird stamps against the grey sky, it seems to be a big rather than a small bird. Some other bird darting across the wires of rain—a swallow or a sparrow— forms a much smaller dot. No, that one up there is not a sparrow, nor even a pigeon. With tempestuous flight it has dived down, revealing points of light in between the feathers of its fringed wings. It turns upon itself to peck at its seemingly long tail, using the branch as a swing. If you watch it attentively, it grows in size and the tangle of boughs is hardly noticed any more. It is a gigantic tree and must be centuries old; from how many hundreds of windows can it be observed? Perhaps no one except me has noticed the celestial visitor; or perhaps they have. For if I happen to prick my inner ear, I catch many other voices unheard before, and which, to be sure, I shall never hear again.

— It's a carrier-pigeon; it's a magpie that has lost its way; it's a duck, — shout almost in a chorus the people living on the fourteenth floor of a brick-red skyscraper.

— Could it be a kestrel? But I don't see its beak. Give me the binoculars, Adalgisa — says the naturalist, nestled in a penthouse in Via Borgospesso.

— The raven of Edgar Poe — says the old painter in Via Bigli 17, who had illustrated the poem some thirty years ago.

— Thou wast not born for death, immortal bird — observes a bald man from the attic of Via Pietro Verri, who had twice failed the final exams in English literature that would have qualified him to become a university teacher. — Who wrote those words? Keats or Shelley? Pasqualina, give me that yellow book on the fireplace, please. Skylark? Or nightingale? But that bird is as big as a hen. 'Thou wast not born for death'. . . . Oh, damn it. To think that it was on this very poem that they harassed me in the exam.

— It looks like a peacock. But how on earth could he get over there? — says a butler in Via Sant'Andrea. — Come, have a look at it, Annetta; come, don't be so squeamish, stay with me a while; the master and the mistress are out anyway. Have you ever eaten a peacock?

A more confused sound, a smack (perhaps a kiss?) a little argument. — It's a hawk! — says a female voice coming from a roof behind that of my house. — A young hawk, happy . . . and free. He can go wherever he wishes. He's not bothered by the storm; he does not know what bothers, engagements, worries, mean. He flies and lives. In a little while he will be at Codogno, then at Parma, and then in Sicily. He alights on a tree and no one asks him to show his identity card. He eats what is there to eat—grass, mice, insects; and he drinks an elixir of rose-leaves sweeter than Chablis. He is a God clothed in feathers, but still a God. It's a hawk, I tell you. I wish I were him.

— Are you crazy? — says a man's voice, who must be standing beside her — the hawks live in the mountains and one day they are stuffed and so they aren't happy at all. I bet that's only a jay, a poor old jay that perhaps in a few hours' time will be killed by a hunter. Moreover, it's inedible. What are you mumbling? That one hour of freedom is better than a whole lifetime of slavery? Silly romanticism! Can't you see that if you don't go to the office—on Sundays, for instance— you feel out of your element, and feel yourself to be more dead than alive. Man creates innumerable obligations for himself, and plunges himself into a sea of troubles in order to enjoy the pleasure of overcoming them. He cultivates his own unhappiness so that he may have the satisfaction of struggling piecemeal against it. To be always unhappy, but not too much, is the indispensable condition of these brief and intermittent periods of happiness. Am I talking like a professor? Silly woman! What would you do over there, at the top of that tree, wet to the skin and . . . without me? Perhaps you would like to leave for Codogno? Or for Sicily? Would you not? Have you got the nerve to say so? Just try, silly girl! Fly! Try to fly!

A gust of wind shakes the windowpanes as well as the tree. With a sudden start the hawk takes off from the branch, stands out against the sky like a heraldic emblem, then dives down amidst the lofty roofs and disappears. Then starts its flight over again. The branch it had perched on keeps swaying for some time. It's pouring harder and harder. Indistinct voices of people holding out an argument reach me, and I can make out the familiar voice of a man saying:

—You are right, I apologise; it was a hawk; a strong, free and wonderful hawk. You wish you were him . . . and I can understand that. I wish so too . . . but with you. And that's the difference—a slight difference. What are you saying? That it isn't a slight difference after all? It was a hawk, I'm sorry; don't know why I took it into my head to deny that. I, who know so little about birds. He will be at Casalpusterlengo by now, or perhaps flying over the Po. I admit it was a hawk, and you were right. . . . I beg your forgiveness . . . yes please. . . .

Another gust, some strange sound (perhaps a kiss). And then the last faint voice:

— With milk or lemon? I never remember. We stay so little at home. . . . A beautiful bird, no doubt. I think it has reached Piacenza by now and is flying over Piazza dei Cavalli.

The Snow Statue

It's cold, Saint Moritz is buried in snow, the radiator is working
marvellously, and I am strolling (in my rooms) in pyjamas. I
don't ski, skate or go on excursions; nor do I sleigh; I find
the mountains boring in summer and quite unbearable in
winter. At the end of the year I come to this place to see the
ballet organised by my friend Kind, to receive a cardboard
donkey, a toy trumpet, a paper hat, or any sort of trifle; and
lastly to enjoy the sight of families clinging to each other as
the champagne corks shoot off. But the main reason for my
coming here is to see the statue or enormous puppet of snow
made by Mr. S. right in front of his hotel, which is just opposite
mine. From my window I enjoy the spectacle of this snowman
—nine feet tall, with a plumed hat, a cigar in his mouth with
the ash about to fall, two carrots for ears, two onions as eyes
and three turnips as the buttons of his jacket. He partly re-
sembles Churchill and partly Grock. But what attracts me
most is the onion-eyes. From the very first day they have called
forth in me, by association of ideas, the most lugubrious
of sentiments. One thing is certain: the enormous bogey is
crying. He is the only person here, in these days of festivity,
who can really cry. He sheds red, pungent tears—huge drops,
like billiard-balls. But no one sees his tears except me. He is
not the same bogey as of past years, but a new one made
for this year; and yet it's always the same to me. If he cries,
it is not simply because he has onions in his eye-sockets, but
for reasons that I can't explain and that I find pointless to
probe. And when he is wrapped up in a bundle by a fresh
drizzle of snow, and his eyes become more bleared and floury,
he doesn't resemble Churchill any more, only Grock. He seems
to say: 'Are you having a nice time? Enjoy yourselves. I
weep for all of you, while I wait to be dissolved and to cast
these onions into the slushy mud of the road.'

I have never met Moby Dick, the white whale, but I have

seen Grock many a time, and (standing by the window, tarnished by my breath) I try to speak to this wonderful puppet: — May I, Maestro, join you in your unrestrainable, total and universal weeping? I have come here on purpose to see you; although I am not worthy of such an honour, I am perhaps the only person here who knows why you cry. I would also dissolve into your mud; I too have onions in my eye-sockets, a turnip instead of a nose. . . . May I, Maestro—?

A light tap on the door and the maid comes in with the tea. She is a Tuscan, matter-of-fact and not much given to mysticism.

— Have you seen it? — she asks me, seeing me absorbed by the window. — They've made another scarecrow this year.

— Oh yes — I answer in an indifferent way. — That big puppet. Why on earth did they do so?

The Butterfly of Dinard

Would the tiny saffron-coloured butterfly, which used to come to see me every day at the café in the square of Dinard, and bring me word about you—or so it seemed—visit that cold windy little square again after I left? It was incredible that the chilly Breton summer should have brought out so many sparks, all the same colour, in those benumbed kitchen gardens. Perhaps what I had seen was not just butterflies, but *the* butterfly of Dinard. And I was curious to learn if the morning visitor turned up regularly just for my sake, deliberately ignoring other cafés in preference to the one ('Les Cornouailles') which I used to frequent, or if this cosy little corner merely happened to be listed in its daily mechanical itinerary. Was it, in short, a morning walk, or a secret message? To resolve this doubt I decided to give, before leaving, a handsome tip to the waitress, together with my address in Italy. She was to write to me and tell me if the visitor had come again, or if it had disappeared. I waited for the butterfly to perch on the vase, and then took out a hundred-franc note, a pencil and a piece of paper, and called for the waitress. Stammering in more than usually shaky French, I tried to explain the situation—not, of course, the whole, but only part of it. I gave her to understand that I was an entomologist, and that I was interested to know if the butterfly would come back again to the café after I had left, and how long it could survive in this bitter cold. By the time I'd finished explaining I was exhausted and terrified.

— A butterfly?— asked the charming Filli, with her eyes *alla Greuze* — On that vase? No Monsieur, I don't see anything. Please look again. Merci bien, Monsieur.

She pocketed the note and went away carrying the coffee percolator. I bent my head, and when I raised it again, there was no butterfly on the vase of dahlias.